A+
Practice Tests

Michael A. Pastore

A+ Practice Tests Exam Cram

Limits of Liability and Disclaimer of Warranty

Trademarks

The Coriolis Group, LLC
14455 N. Hayden Road
Suite 220
Scottsdale, Arizona 85260

(480)483-0192
FAX (480)483-0193
www.coriolis.com

Library of Congress Cataloging-in-Publication Data
Pastore, Michael A.
    A+ practice tests / by Michael A. Pastore.--2nd ed.
        p.   cm. -- (Exam cram)
    ISBN 1-58880-264-7
    1. Electronic data processing personnel--Certification.   2. Computer technicians--Certification--Study guides.   I. Title.   II. Series.
QA76.3.P37   2001
621.39'16'076--dc21   2001047754
                                                              CIP

Printed in the United States of America
10 9 8 7 6 5 4 3 2 1

President and CEO
Roland Elgey

Publisher
Al Valvano

Associate Publisher
Katherine R. Hartlove

Acquisitions Editor
Sharon Linsenbach

Product Marketing Manager
Jeff Johnson

Project Editor
Dan Young

Technical Reviewer
Diana Bartley

Production Coordinator
Wendy Littley

Cover Designer
Jesse Dunn

CD-ROM Developer
Michelle McConnell

The Coriolis Group, LLC • 14455 North Hayden Road, Suite 220 • Scottsdale, Arizona 85260

A Note from Coriolis

Our goal has always been to provide you with the best study tools on the planet to help you achieve your certification in record time. Time is so valuable these days that none of us can afford to waste a second of it, especially when it comes to exam preparation.

Over the past few years, we've created an extensive line of *Exam Cram* and *Exam Prep* study guides, practice exams, and interactive training. To help you study even better, we have now created an e-learning and certification destination called **ExamCram.com**. (You can access the site at **www.examcram.com**.) Now, with every study product you purchase from us, you'll be connected to a large community of people like yourself who are actively studying for their certifications, developing their careers, seeking advice, and sharing their insights and stories.

We believe that the future is all about collaborative learning. Our **ExamCram.com** destination is our approach to creating a highly interactive, easily accessible collaborative environment, where you can take practice exams and discuss your experiences with others, sign up for features like "Questions of the Day," plan your certifications using our interactive planners, create your own personal study pages, and keep up with all of the latest study tips and techniques.

We hope that whatever study products you purchase from us—*Exam Cram* or *Exam Prep* study guides, *Personal Trainers, Personal Test Centers*, or one of our interactive Web courses—will make your studying fun and productive. Our commitment is to build the kind of learning tools that will allow you to study the way you want to, whenever you want to.

Visit ExamCram.com now to enhance your study program.

Help us continue to provide the very best certification study materials possible. Write us or email us at **learn@examcram.com** and let us know how our study products have helped you study. Tell us about new features that you'd like us to add. Send us a story about how we've helped you. We're listening!

Good luck with your certification exam and your career. Thank you for allowing us to help you achieve your goals.

ExamCram.com **Connects You to the Ultimate Study Center!**

Look for these other products from The Coriolis Group:

A+ Exam Cram, Second Edition
By James Jones and Craig Landes

Linux+ Exam Cram
By Michael Jang

Server+ Exam Prep
By Drew Bird and Mike Harwood

PC Technician Black Book
By Ron Gilster

Also recently published by Coriolis Certification Insider Press:

CCNA Exam Cram, Third Edition
By Sheldon Barry

CCSA Exam Cram
By Tony Piltzecker

Server+ Exam Cram
By Deborah Haralson and Jeff Haralson

This book is dedicated to all of you who work tirelessly into the night to get ahead in life. Choosing to do better with your life is a terrific way to invest your time and effort. A career can take many paths; you start down a road towards your goals and you will be given opportunities to explore and grow as an individual. You choosing to become A+ certified is a great way to start down a new path.

I also dedicate this book to Sheryl, my wife, who has always encouraged me to follow my heart and has stuck by me no matter what.

❧

About the Author

Michael A. Pastore is the President of LightPoint Learning Solutions, a Microsoft Certified Solution Provider and Certified Technical Education Center. LightPoint has its headquarters in Bellevue, Washington, and has several training center locations including Phoenix, Arizona, and Long Beach, California.

For over 20 years, Michael has been an active instructor, teacher, and consultant in the computer field. He has performed in a number of different capacities in the IT industry including Network Administrator, help-desk professional, and systems integrator and consultant. He has a Masters Degree in Leadership and Management from City University. Michael teaches both business and technology courses for the University of Phoenix.

Michael is A+ and Network+ certified and has been involved for several years in a number of CompTIA initiatives on certification and training.

Acknowledgments

This book is made possible by the work of a number of individuals.

First, I'd like to thank Randall Thomas for his help in getting the initial work done.

I also want to thank everyone at The Coriolis Group who was instrumental in creating this product, including Sharon Linsenbach, Dan Young, Wendy Littley, Jennifer Ashley, Diana Bartley, and Jesse Dunn.

Table of Contents

Introduction xi

Chapter 1
A+ Core Hardware Practice Test #1 1

Chapter 2
A+ Core Hardware Answer Key #1 21

Chapter 3
A+ Core Hardware Practice Test #2 45

Chapter 4
A+ Core Hardware Answer Key #2 67

Chapter 5
A+ OS Technologies Practice Test #1 91

Chapter 6
A+ OS Technologies Answer Key #1 113

Chapter 7
A+ OS Technologies Practice Test #2 133

Chapter 8
A+ OS Technologies Answer Key #2 157

Introduction

You Spoke

Welcome to *A+ Practice Tests Exam Cram, 2nd Edition*! A survey of Coriolis readers showed us how important practice questions are in your efforts to prepare to take and pass certification exams. You asked us to give you more practice tests on a variety of certification topics, including MCSE Core Four, MCSE+I, A+, Network+, and others.

We Responded

The *Practice Tests Exam Cram* series is our answer to your requests, and provides you with entirely new practice tests for many certification topics. Each practice test appears in its own chapter, followed by a corresponding answer and explanation chapter, in the same format as the Sample Test and Answer Key chapters at the end of each of our *Exam Cram* books. We not only tell you which answers are correct, but we also explain why the right answers are right and why the wrong answers are wrong. That's because we're convinced that you can learn as much from understanding the wrong answers as you can from knowing the right ones!

This book makes a perfect companion to any study material you may own that covers the exam subject matter. For those of you who already own *A+ Exam Cram, 2nd Edition*, we have included a time-saving study feature. At the end of each answer, you will find a reference to the *Exam Cram* book. That way, if you want to review the material on which the question is based in more depth, you will be able to quickly locate that information.

But Wait, There's More!

This book also includes a CD-ROM that contains two more exams, one on each of the A+ test modules: Core Hardware and Operating System Technologies. In addition, all four of the exams in the book are also on the CD.

Thus, this book and CD give you access to a pool of 210 questions for each of the exams, for a total of 420 questions. Thorough review of these materials should provide you with a reasonably complete view of the numerous topics and types of questions you're likely to see on the real CompTIA A+ exams. Because questions come and go on CompTIA exams pretty regularly, we can't claim total coverage, but we have designed these question pools to deal with the topics and concepts that are most likely to appear on a real exam in some form or fashion.

Using This Book to Prepare for an Exam

You should begin your preparation process by working through the questions in the book to guide your studies. As you discover topics or concepts that may be unfamiliar or unclear, be sure to consult additional study materials to increase your knowledge and familiarity with the materials involved. In fact, you should employ this particular technique on any practice test questions you come across that may expose areas in your knowledge base that may need further development or elaboration.

To help you increase your knowledge base, we suggest that you work with whatever materials you have at hand. Certainly, we can't help but recommend our own *A+ Exam Cram, 2nd Edition* and *A+ Exam Prep, 3rd Edition* books, but you will find that both these resources cite numerous other sources of information as well. Several very good reference books exist that you may find helpful in preparing for the exam.

Once you've worked your way through the practice tests in the book, use the exams on the CD-ROM to assess your test readiness. That way, you can build confidence in your ability to sit for and pass these exams, as you master the subject material for each one.

We recommend you shoot for a 75 percent score when you take the practice tests. If you don't make the grade, you probably should take some low-cost practice exams from commercial vendors. Use these practice exams to increase your knowledge, familiarity, and understanding of the materials involved in the topic area, rather than spending the money on a CompTIA test that you may not pass. Because each CompTIA exam costs between $85 and $120, we think you're better off spending some of that money on more preparation, and saving what you can to help pay for the exam when you're really ready to pass it!

Tell Us What You Think

Feel free to share your feedback on the book with us. We'll carefully consider your comments. Please be sure to include the title of the book in your message; otherwise, we'll be forced to guess which book you are writing about. Please send your comments and questions to us at **learn@examcram.com**.

Visit our Web site at **www.examcram.com** for the latest on what's happening in the world of certification, updates, and new *Exam Prep* and *Exam Cram* titles. For the latest information on CompTIA certification exams, visit CompTIA's Web site at **www.comptia.org**. Good luck with your exams!

A+ Core Hardware Practice Test #1

Question 1

Which expansion card would you normally use in a portable PC?

○ a. PC Card

○ b. ISA

○ c. PCI

○ d. MCA

Question 2

Why would you install the back tabs in a PC system? [Choose the two best answers]

❏ a. Airflow

❏ b. ESD

❏ c. Surge suppression

❏ d. Dust prevention

Question 3

An ISA card would normally work in which expansion ports? [Choose the two best answers]

❑ a. PCI

❑ b. ISA

❑ c. EISA

❑ d. Card Bus

Question 4

Which device is IRQ 1 normally associated with?

○ a. Keyboard

○ b. Mouse

○ c. COM1

○ d. COM2

Question 5

Which device is IRQ 3 normally associated with?

○ a. COM1

○ b. LPT1

○ c. COM2

○ d. System timer

Question 6

The port that is normally associated with the printer end of a printer cable is:

○ a. Centronics 36-pin connector

○ b. DB-25 male

○ c. DB-15 female

○ d. USB

Question 7

What is the memory address used for COM1?

○ a. 03F8

○ b. 2EF8

○ c. 3CF8

○ d. 2CF8

Question 8

ZIF sockets refer to which type of connection?

○ a. Memory

○ b. CMOS

○ c. CPU

○ d. I/O Port

Question 9

Which type of connector is normally associated with the computer side of a printer cable?

○ a. DB-25 male

○ b. DB-25 female

○ c. DB-9 male

○ d. Centronics 36-pin connector

Question 10

An external modem is normally connected to which type of connector on a PC system?

○ a. DB-15 male

○ b. DB-9 female

○ c. DB-9 male

○ d. DB-25 female

Question 11

The *dot pitch* of .28 refers to which monitor characteristic?

○ a. .28 mm dot width of a pixel

○ b. .28 cm dot width of a pixel

○ c. .28 mm distance between pixels

○ d. .28 cm distance between pixels

Question 12

What is the standard resolution of a VGA monitor?

○ a. 480×120

○ b. 640×480

○ c. 1024×510

○ d. 80×40

Question 13

If the battery on the motherboard fails, which will be affected? [Choose the two best answers]

❑ a. ROM

❑ b. CMOS

❑ c. System clock

❑ d. RAM

Question 14

A 9-pin male connector on the back of a PC is usually related to the:

○ a. Video port

○ b. Printer port

○ c. Monitor port

○ d. Serial port

Question 15

A SIMM port on a motherboard is used for:

○ a. Memory

○ b. Video

○ c. Card expansion

○ d. Voltage regulation

Question 16

You are a customer-service technician and you have received a call from a customer indicating that his/her system passes the memory test but hangs up before CMOS Setup. Which component has likely failed?

○ a. CPU

○ b. Memory

○ c. Video card

○ d. Expansion card

Question 17

Which of the following types of memory are normally associated with video memory? [Choose the two best answers]

❑ a. SIMM

❑ b. SDRAM

❑ c. VRAM

❑ d. WRAM

Question 18

You have just installed a new sound card in a customer's PC. The system passes the self-test normally but does not boot. Which of the following is most likely the problem?

○ a. Defective sound card

○ b. Improper IRQ settings on the sound card

○ c. Memory failure

○ d. Speaker connections are not correct

Question 19

You are replacing a motherboard on a PC system. Which of the following must be checked before installing the new motherboard?

○ a. Exact motherboard replacement type

○ b. Exact motherboard model number

○ c. AT power connection compatibility

○ d. Exact video board compatibility

Question 20

PCI cards provide which of the following capabilities? [Choose the two best answers]

❏ a. plug-and-play

❏ b. 16-bit data width

❏ c. Power saver functionality

❏ d. Hardware jumpers for maximum configuration flexibility

Question 21

Which of the following connectors are normally used for keyboard or mouse connections? [Choose the two best answers]

A   B   C   D

- ❑ a. Connector A
- ❑ b. Connector B
- ❑ c. Connector C
- ❑ d. Connector D

Question 22

Which of the following is the pin configuration for a letter-quality dot-matrix printer?

- ○ a. 24-pin
- ○ b. 9-pin
- ○ c. 36-pin
- ○ d. 15-pin

Question 23

A laser printer uses which type of process for image transfer?

- ○ a. EP process
- ○ b. OP process
- ○ c. Impact method
- ○ d. Nozzle-jet

Question 24

You are installing a legacy network card into a PC. The card has jumpers for configuration options. These jumpers are most likely for configuring which options? [Choose the three best answers]

❑ a. MAC address

❑ b. IRQ settings

❑ c. DMA settings

❑ d. Memory address settings

Question 25

You are trying to troubleshoot a PC COM port problem. Which device would you normally use for this process?

○ a. Null-modem cable

○ b. Loop back connector

○ c. COM terminator plug

○ d. Voltmeter

Question 26

Most modems use which command functions?

○ a. Hayes-compatible

○ b. TFTP protocol

○ c. FTP protocol

○ d. URL commands

Question 27

ESD is a primary concern in which type of environment?

○ a. High humidity/Low temperature

○ b. High humidity/High temperature

○ c. Low humidity/High temperature

○ d. Low humidity/Low temperature

Question 28

An Ultra Wide SCSI connection can normally have which number of devices attached to it?

- ○ a. 8
- ○ b. 7
- ○ c. 15
- ○ d. 32

Question 29

When installing a SCSI device on a bus, which things must be known for proper operation? [Choose the two best answers]

- ❑ a. ID
- ❑ b. Voltage
- ❑ c. Termination (internal or external)
- ❑ d. MAC address

Question 30

Ink jet printers transfer images to paper using which following method?

- ○ a. Heat bonding
- ○ b. Nozzle and ink spray
- ○ c. EP process
- ○ d. PO process

Question 31

What is the standard measurement for printer image quality?

- ○ a. DPI
- ○ b. CPI
- ○ c. LPI
- ○ d. RPI

Question 32

Drive C: is normally reserved for which type of device?

○ a. Floppy disk

○ b. CD-ROM

○ c. Hard drive

○ d. DVD

Question 33

A CD-ROM is readable by which types of devices? [Choose the two best answers]

❑ a. Floppy disk

❑ b. CD-ROM drive

❑ c. DVD drive

❑ d. Zip drive

Question 34

What is the standard resolution for SVGA?

○ a. 640×480

○ b. 800×600

○ c. 512×1024

○ d. 1024×768

Question 35

Which of the following installation errors will probably damage an ISA drive?

○ a. Installing the control cable backward

○ b. Configuring the Master/Slave jumper incorrectly

○ c. Installing the power cable upside down

○ d. Forcing the control cable onto the drive

Question 36

What is the typical storage capacity of a CD-ROM?

○ a. 1.2MB

○ b. 360KB

○ c. 650MB

○ d. 5120MB

Question 37

The last device in a SCSI chain must be a:

○ a. Truncator

○ b. Concatonator

○ c. Terminator

○ d. Floppy drive

Question 38

The command to hang up a Hayes compatible modem is:

○ a. ATZ

○ b. ATH

○ c. ATDT

○ d. ATM

Question 39

What is the normal bus speed of a Pentium 200?

○ a. 66MHz

○ b. 33MHz

○ c. 200MHz

○ d. 400MHz

Question 40

The system front panel lights are active, the disk drive access light comes on, but the system did not beep when turned on. The startup of the operating system appears to be normal. What is the most likely problem?

○ a. Video monitor failure

○ b. Memory module failure

○ c. Video adapter failure

○ d. System speaker is disconnected

Question 41

A customer complains that after installing the operating system on the hard drive, the system will not boot from the hard drive. What are the most likely problems? [Choose the two best answers]

❑ a. Non-bootable media is installed.

❑ b. The boot sequence is incorrect.

❑ c. The drive has developed a malfunction.

❑ d. The power supply has failed.

Question 42

Which type of problem is indicated by a "Press F1 to Continue" message during boot up?

○ a. CMOS error

○ b. Disk error

○ c. Video problem

○ d. Memory problem

Question 43

A 301 error message indicates which type of failure?

- ○ a. Memory problem
- ○ b. Keyboard problem
- ○ c. Video problem
- ○ d. Multimedia problem

Question 44

The printer port and network card in a PC system are intermittently malfunctioning. What is the most likely problem?

- ○ a. IRQ conflicts
- ○ b. MAC address conflicts
- ○ c. Defective video card
- ○ d. Memory problems

Question 45

The USB port allows for the connection of devices using a device called a:

- ○ a. Hub
- ○ b. Post box
- ○ c. Router
- ○ d. Terminator

Question 46

Which event occurs when a computer is first turned on?

- ○ a. POST
- ○ b. IPL
- ○ c. Interrupts are loaded
- ○ d. Plug-and-play is configured

Question 47

A 10BaseT network requires which type of wiring as a minimum?

O a. CAT 5

O b. CAT 3

O c. CAT 1

O d. Fiber-optic cable

Question 48

You want to add a third disk drive to a machine with only one IDE controller on it. What would you do to add this drive?

O a. Connect it to the floppy channel.

O b. This is not possible under any circumstances.

O c. Only install it on the provided cables.

O d. Install a second IDE controller.

Question 49

You are installing a CD-ROM onto a system that has two disk drives. Each disk drive is attached to an IDE channel. How could you do this?

O a. Connect the CD-ROM as a master on the second IDE port.

O b. Connect the CD-ROM as a master on the primary IDE port.

O c. Connect the CD-ROM as slave on the second IDE port.

O d. Install the CD-ROM onto the floppy channel.

Question 50

The system time is stored during power off in which of the following?

O a. CMOS

O b. ROM

O c. RAM

O d. The system time is not stored.

Question 51

Video monitors are typically installed onto which connector?

- ○ a. Connector A
- ○ b. Connector B
- ○ c. Connector C
- ○ d. Connector D

Question 52

Which type of RAM is typically used for caching?

- ○ a. VRAM
- ○ b. SRAM
- ○ c. DRAM
- ○ d. CMOS

Question 53

Which of these are standard designations for cache memory? [Choose the two best answers]

- ❑ a. L1
- ❑ b. L2
- ❑ c. C1
- ❑ d. C2

Question 54

During startup your computer gives you a 1701 error message. What does this signify?

○ a. Keyboard failure

○ b. Hard drive controller failure

○ c. CPU failure

○ d. NMI failure

Question 55

Dust accumulation in a computer system causes which type of problem?

○ a. Heat dissipation

○ b. ESD

○ c. I/O channel clatter

○ d. Disk head crashes

Question 56

You have been called onto the site of a computer that is malfunctioning. Upon examination, you discover that the case is open and that boards have been swapped. Several boards are lying on the floor and the computer is running. How would you go about troubleshooting the system at this point?

○ a. Put all the boards back in the system and identify the malfunction.

○ b. Install the boards one at a time until the system malfunctions.

○ c. Refuse to work on the system until the customer puts the system back together.

○ d. Call a supervisor and seek higher direction.

Question 57

The floppy drive of a computer system seems to be malfunctioning. The customer indicates that he was trying to install a new hard drive. The floppy drive read activity light is permanently on, and the drive is spinning but it will not boot. What is the most likely problem with this system?

- a. The floppy disk has malfunctioned.
- b. The control cable for the floppy has been installed backward.
- c. The IDE controller has been shorted out.
- d. The new hard drive is defective.

Question 58

The device that translates network protocol from one type to another is called a:

- a. Router
- b. Gateway
- c. Hub
- d. Bypass connector

Question 59

You are troubleshooting a computer that continually passes the POST but will not boot the hard drive. When you put a bootable CD-ROM into the computer, the CD-ROM boots correctly and seems to work. You have checked the BIOS settings and determined that the boot sequence is C:, CD-ROM, floppy. The drive activity light is not blinking and the drive does not appear to be spinning. Which of the following might be the problem? [Choose the three best answers]

- a. Power is not properly connected to the hard drive.
- b. The system power supply has malfunctioned.
- c. The control cable for the hard drive has been reversed.
- d. The Master/Slave connection is configured improperly.

Question 60

Which of the following use a 15-pin male connector on the cable?

○ a. Serial port

○ b. Printer port

○ c. USB port

○ d. Monitor connection

Question 61

A SCSI chain requires a terminator in which of the following locations? [Choose the two best answers]

❏ a. At the head of the SCSI chain.

❏ b. At the end of the SCSI chain.

❏ c. On each device in the chain.

❏ d. SCSI chains do not require termination.

Question 62

You want to add a USB device to your computer system. In order to do this, you will need to do which of the following?

○ a. Power off the system to install the device.

○ b. Plug the device into the USB port.

○ c. Reset the BIOS.

○ d. Reformat the hard drive.

Question 63

You want to connect a serial mouse to your system. Which of the following must be checked? [Choose the two best answers]

❏ a. A COM port is available for the mouse.

❏ b. The PS/2 mouse is disconnected.

❏ c. The port is not connected to any other devices.

❏ d. The computer is powered off.

Question 64

A successful POST is indicated by which of the following?

○ a. One beep

○ b. Two beeps

○ c. Three beeps

○ d. Four beeps

Question 65

You want to swap a PC Card device in a portable computer. To do this, you must turn the computer off.

○ a. True

○ b. False

Question 66

You want to upgrade the BIOS on desktop computer. You download the upgrade from the manufacturer's Web site onto a floppy disk. Before you continue, you should do which of the following?

○ a. Verify that the computer is running on batteries.

○ b. Verify that the computer is running on the power supply.

○ c. Reset the BIOS to default settings.

○ d. Disconnect the CMOS battery on the computer.

Question 67

A cold boot causes the computer to do which of the following first?

○ a. Run POST.

○ b. Perform an initial program load.

○ c. Load operating system.

○ d. Verify NMI configuration.

Question 68

You have just installed a multimedia card in a desktop computer. What three settings must be confirmed when you turn the system on?

○ a. Port number, MAC address, IRQ

○ b. IRQ, DMA, I/O address

○ c. Himem, I/O address, IRQ

○ d. DMA, Himem, IRQ

Question 69

You powered a computer on and received a message indicating 1701 followed by "Press F1 to Continue." This is an indication of which type of problem? [Choose the two best answers]

❑ a. Disk drive controller error

❑ b. POST

❑ c. Video

❑ d. Memory

Question 70

You are troubleshooting a system that is behaving improperly. While removing expansion cards, the system suddenly begins working properly. What can you assume?

○ a. The power supply is defective.

○ b. The floppy drive is defective.

○ c. The component you just removed is defective.

○ d. The motherboard is defective.

A+ Core Hardware
Answer Key #1

1. a	19. a	37. c	55. a
2. a, d	20. a, c	38. b	56. b
3. b, c	21. a, b	39. a	57. b
4. a	22. a	40. d	58. b
5. c	23. a	41. a, b	59. a, c, d
6. a	24. b, c, d	42. a	60. d
7. a	25. b	43. b	61. a, b
8. c	26. a	44. a	62. b
9. a	27. d	45. a	63. a, d
10. c	28. c	46. a	64. a
11. c	29. a, c	47. b	65. b
12. b	30. b	48. d	66. b
13. b, c	31. a	49. c	67. a
14. d	32. c	50. a	68. b
15. a	33. b, c	51. d	69. a, b
16. d	34. b	52. b	70. c
17. c, d	35. d	53. a, b	
18. b	36. c	54. b	

Question 1

The correct answer is a. PC Cards are normally used on laptops and portable systems. Answer b is incorrect because Industry Standard Architecture (ISA) expansion cards are usually found only on older desktop PC systems. Answer c is incorrect because Peripheral Component Interconnect (PCI) is the current expansion port on PC desktop and larger systems. Answer d is incorrect because Micro Channel Architecture (MCA) is an interface typically only found on IBM PS/2 systems.

For more information on this topic, see *A+ Exam Cram, 2nd Edition*, Chapter 2, the section "Expansion Bus Architecture".

Question 2

The correct answers are a and d. The tabs on the back of the system case are important because they help keep airflow over the motherboard and help prevent dust from entering the case. Answer b is incorrect because Electro Static Discharge (ESD) is primarily an atmospheric phenomena and not associated with metal enclosed components like a motherboard. Answer c is incorrect because the tabs on the expansion case do not help address surge suppression. Power surges are a function of input line voltages and are usually handled by either a surge suppresser or a universal power supply (UPS).

For more information on this topic, see *A+ Exam Cram, 2nd Edition*, Chapter 2, the section "Components of the Motherboard".

Question 3

The correct answers are b and c. ISA cards work in ISA slots as well as in EISA slots (in most cases). ISA cards are only guaranteed to work in ISA expansion ports. ISA cards are supposed to work in EISA slots and usually do. Answer a is incorrect because PCI slots are not compatible with ISA slots. Answer d is incorrect for the same reason as answer a. PC Card is used extensively portable and laptop machines, ISA has not been available in portable systems for several years. PCI is a fast data transfer bus and a PC Card is used for portable and laptop computers. You may encounter PCI slot capability in some portable environments, but it is extremely rare.

For more information on this topic, see *A+ Exam Cram, 2nd Edition*, Chapter 2, the section "Expansion Bus Architecture".

Question 4

The correct answer is a. IRQ 1 is always associated with the keyboard. Answer b is incorrect because the mouse typically uses IRQ 11 or IRQ 12. Answer c is incorrect because COM1 uses IRQ 4 by default. Answer d is incorrect because COM2 will usually be set to IRQ 3 by default. PCI solves or greatly simplifies IRQ problems because you can set all of the PCI expansion cards to the same IRQ. This simplifies installation on systems that are largely full.

For more information on this topic, see *A+ Exam Cram, 2nd Edition*, Chapter 5, the section "IRQs, DMA, and I/O Ports".

Question 5

The correct answer is c. The COM2 default is set to IRQ 3. Answer a is incorrect because COM1 is set to IRQ 4. Answer b is incorrect as LPT1 is usually set to IRQ 7. Answer d is incorrect; the system timer is set to IRQ 0.

For more information on this topic, see *A+ Exam Cram, 2nd Edition*, Chapter 5, the section "IRQs, DMA, and I/O Ports".

Question 6

The correct answer is a. This question is a bit tricky because it concerns the cable end, not the printer. Answer b is incorrect because DB-25 would normally be associated with the computer end of the cable. Answer c is incorrect because DB-15 connections are used for older video monitor connections. Answer d is incorrect, because USB, while now available on many printers, does not have a special printer cable. USB devices use a generic USB cable.

For more information on this topic, see *A+ Exam Cram, 2nd Edition*, Chapter 7, the section "Printers".

Question 7

The correct answer is a. 03F8 is the memory address used for COM1. Answer b is incorrect because COM2 uses 02F8. Answers c and d are incorrect because 3CF8 and 2CF8 are not valid address assignments for devices.

For more information on this topic, see *A+ Exam Cram, 2nd Edition*, Chapter 5, the section "IRQs, DMA, and I/O Ports".

Question 8

The correct answer is c. Zero Insertion Force (ZIF) sockets are used almost exclusively for CPU and other high-density chips. ZIF sockets allow for the installation of the processor with a minimal risk of damaging a pin on the CPU. Answer a is incorrect because memory will use either a Dual Inline Memory Module/Single Inline Memory Module (DIMM/SIMM) or other similar type of connection. Answer b is incorrect; Complementary Metal Oxide Semiconductor (CMOS) is generally a ROM-type chip and is usually either a Dual In Line Pin (DIP) type of layout, or permanently soldered onto the motherboard. Answer d is incorrect because input/output (I/O) ports are hardwired connections on virtually all PC systems.

For more information on this topic, see *A+ Exam Cram, 2nd Edition*, Chapter 2, the section "Slots and Sockets".

Question 9

The correct answer is a. The DB-25 male connector is the connector associated with the computer side of the printer cable. The DB-25 male is connected to the DB-25 female connector on the back of the system unit. Answer b is incorrect because the DB-25 female connector is on the computer case, and the printer cable is connected to the connector on the case. Answer c is also wrong because the DB-9 connectors are exclusively associated with serial communications ports. Answer d is wrong because on PC systems the printer side of the connector is associated with the Centronics connector, not the computer side.

You will, however, find that some computer systems will have a Centronics connector on the case. This might be a printer connection, or it could be a SCSI connection. One more twist you should be aware of is that many non-PC systems use the DB-25 as it was originally intended—for serial communications.

For more information on this topic, see *A+ Exam Cram, 2nd Edition*, Chapter 7, the section "Printers".

Question 10

The correct answer is c. A DB-9 male connector will be associated with the back panel of a PC for communications. DB-9 connectors may have either a DB-9 connector or a DB-25 connector on the other end, depending on the type of cable purchased and its use. Some older external modems still use a DB-25 pin connector for the computer connection. Answer a is incorrect because the DB-15 connectors are usually associated with monitor connections. Answer b is incorrect because the A DB-9 female connector is what would be on the cable that connects to the computer DB-9 connection. Answer d is incorrect because the DB-25 connectors on the back of a computer are used for printer ports.

For more information on this topic, see *A+ Exam Cram, 2nd Edition*, Chapter 9, the section "Serial (COM) Ports: 1 Bit after Another".

Question 11

The correct answer is c. The measure of dot pitch refers to the distance of width between pixels. A standard dot pitch is .28 mm. Generally, the lower the dot pitch the better the monitor. Answer a is incorrect because the dot width of a pixel is very small and referred to as *pixel width*. Answer b is incorrect because a .28 cm dot width of a pixel would be totally unusable for any kind of monitor. Answer d is incorrect because a .28 cm distance between pixels would make the monitor unusable for anything but very large presentation screens, such as you might see in a large stadium. Dot pitch is a standard monitor characteristic you would use in evaluating monitor quality. Most good monitors have a dot pitch of .25mm to .28mm.

For more information on this topic, see *A+ Exam Cram, 2nd Edition*, Chapter 7, the section "Video Displays".

Question 12

The correct answer is b. The standard resolution for VGA is 640×480. Early VGA provided by IBM also referenced 320×200 and 256 colors. The default, however, is 640×480 and 16 colors. Most video adapters support additional modes that can vary resolution depending on the configuration of the video card and monitor capabilities. Answer a is incorrect because 480×120 would be a special mode and probably not very useful in most applications. Answer c is incorrect because 1024×510 would also be a special mode. In most instances, a 1024 exceeds the capability of a VGA adapter and monitor. Answer d is incorrect, and you would probably only encounter this number when dealing with the screen width in text mode.

For more information on this topic, see *A+ Exam Cram, 2nd Edition*, Chapter 7, the section "Standard VGA".

Question 13

The correct answers are b and c. The battery on the motherboard powers the CMOS and the system clock. If this battery fails, the system clock will not be saved when the system is powered down. BIOS settings will also be reset to default values. Answer a is incorrect because ROM is permanent memory and is not affected by the battery. Answer d is incorrect because RAM memory is volatile and will not be saved regardless of the battery. It is a good practice to change the battery on a motherboard every year or so.

For more information on this topic, see *A+ Exam Cram, 2nd Edition*, Chapter 2, the section "System Boards: A Brief History".

Question 14

The correct answer is d. The 9-pin connector on the back of the PC is usually for COM1 or COM2. Answer a is incorrect because the 15-pin connector on the back is for a video monitor. Answer c is incorrect because a video port and a monitor port are the same thing. Answer b is incorrect because printer ports usually have a 25-pin connector on the back of the system unit.

For more information on this topic, see *A+ Exam Cram, 2nd Edition*, Chapter 9, the section "Basic I/O Interfaces".

Question 15

The correct answer is a. SIMM slots or ports were used extensively on motherboards for memory a few years ago, but they have not been used on motherboards for several years and the presence of one is a strong indicator of an old motherboard. You may also see SIMM cards on some printers for memory expansion. Answer b is incorrect because video memory is usually part of the video adapter card. Answer c is incorrect because most card expansion slots on modern systems are PCI or ISA. Answer d is incorrect because voltage regulation is a function of the power supply and not associated with any memory functions.

For more information on this topic, see *A+ Exam Cram, 2nd Edition*, Chapter 4, the section "Packing Modules".

Question 16

The correct answer is d. If the system passes a memory check and you can see it on the monitor, most likely the central processing unit (CPU), memory, and video are working properly. Answer a is likely incorrect because the POST is triggered by a command from the CPU. If the POST starts, the CPU will generally be functional. Answer b is incorrect because you saw the memory pass the memory test. Answer c is incorrect because you saw the memory test on the monitor; therefore, the video card is functioning properly. It's probably a safe assumption that one of the expansion buses is hung, which is why the system hung. A quick way to troubleshoot this problem is to remove all the optional expansion cards and see if the system boots. You will probably find that an expansion card has malfunctioned, a resource conflict exists, or the motherboard is defective.

For more information on this topic, see *A+ Exam Cram, 2nd Edition*, Chapter 14, the section "Boot Problems".

Question 17

The correct answers are c and d. VRAM, or Video RAM (random access memory), and Windows RAM (WRAM) are two types of memory used extensively with video memory systems. These will typically be found on the video card, whether PCI or Accelerated Graphics Port (AGP). Video Random Access Memory (VRAM) supports two paths for data, making access very fast. Windows Random Access Memory (WRAM) has a very fast data transfer rate as well as two ports, like VRAM. Answer a is incorrect because you will generally not see SIMM memory on a modern PC system anywhere. Answer b is incorrect because Synchronous Dynamic RAM (SDRAM) is a type of RAM technology that is used for motherboard memory expansion.

For more information on this topic, see *A+ Exam Cram, 2nd Edition*, Chapter 4, the section "Types of RAM".

Question 18

The correct answer is b. IRQ settings can cause a system to hang during boot up. This is especially true in dealing with ISA-type legacy cards. Answer a is also possible, but check for resource conflicts before deciding that the card is defective. Answer c is also wrong because a memory failure will usually be displayed during the memory check. Answer d is incorrect because an improper speaker would not hang the system.

For more information on this topic, see *A+ Exam Cram, 2nd Edition*, Chapter 14, the section "Diagnostics Tools".

Question 19

The correct answer is a. You have several form factors to consider when replacing a motherboard, which are dependent upon the case and power supply connections. If you have a system that will only accept an AT form factor, you will not be able to use an ATX type motherboard. The model number is usually not critical; therefore, answer b is incorrect. Answer c is incorrect: The type of motherboard you are using dictates the power connections. An AT type case will not accept an ATX motherboard and vice versa. Answer d is incorrect; video cards are usually not an issue unless you are replacing a motherboard that does not support an AGP card, and you have an AGP-type video card.

For more information on this topic, see *A+ Exam Cram, 2nd Edition*, Chapter 2, the section "System Boards: A Brief History".

Question 20

The correct answers are a and c. PCI was intended from the beginning to support plug-and-play functionality. PCI cards are 32-bit width and allow for the bus clock to be turned off. This allows for power savings, and the PC can go into suspension or hibernation mode (these modes are also called *standby* or *hibernate*). Answer b is incorrect because PCI has a 32-bit width. Answer d is incorrect because PCI cards and bus do not have jumpers. From a usability and performance perspective, PCI is the all-around best choice today for expansion slots on a desktop machine.

For more information on this topic, see *A+ Exam Cram, 2nd Edition*, Chapter 2, the section "Peripheral Component Interconnect".

Question 21

The correct answers are a and b. Most modern computers use the PS/2 compatible keyboard and mouse connection (answer b). The 5-pin DIN connector is not normally used in modern computers, because DIN-type connectors are much bigger and more bulky; however, it could be used, so answer a is the second correct answer. Answer c is incorrect because the DB-15 connector is used for monitor connections. Answer d is incorrect because the DB-25 is used for printer connections.

For more information on this topic, see *A+ Exam Cram, 2nd Edition*, Chapter 9, the section "Serial (COM) Ports: 1 Bit after Another".

Question 22

The correct answer is a. The current state of the art for dot-matrix printers is 24-pin. The 24-pin printers can do a reasonable job of creating near letter-quality output and printing through multipart forms. Answer b is incorrect because 9-pin will not generally produce letter-quality text. Answer c is incorrect because 36-pin was a resolution not seen in dot-matrix printers. Answer d is incorrect; a 15-pin printer has never been marketed. You will see some older or lower-cost printers that have 9- or 18-pin configurations.

For more information on this topic, see *A+ Exam Cram, 2ⁿᵈ Edition*, Chapter 7, the section "Printers".

Question 23

The correct answer is a. The Electro-Photographic (EP) process is what is used in laser printers. Answer b is incorrect because the OP process is not a printing method. Answer c is incorrect because impact printing is the technology used for printers such as dot-matrix and band-type printers. Answer d is incorrect because nozzle-jet is used for ink jet printers.

For more information on this topic, see *A+ Exam Cram, 2ⁿᵈ Edition*, Chapter 7, the section "Printers".

Question 24

The correct answers are b, c, and d. Many older network cards will provide jumpers for IRQ and DMA settings. Some of these older cards may also have Dual Inline Pin (DIP) switches to set memory addresses. Answer a is incorrect because the MAC address is set by the manufacturer and burned onto a ROM chip on the controller chip. You should replace these types of cards because they are usually very low performance. Most of the newer cards use plug-and-play technology and should be used whenever possible.

For more information on this topic, see *A+ Exam Cram, 2ⁿᵈ Edition*, Chapter 8, the section "Networking Overview".

Question 25

The correct answer is b. Loop back connectors are used to connect the transmit and receive lines together as well as associated control circuitry. This will allow for a complete loop back connection to be made. Most serial ports provide a mechanism called an internal loop back connection, which tests the internal logic of the port, but not the external connections. The loop back connector will test all of the hardware in the circuit and verify proper operation. Answer a is incorrect because a Null-modem cable is a type of cable used to connect two data COM devices together. Answer c is incorrect because there is no such thing as a COM terminator plug. Answer d is incorrect because a voltmeter would generally not be useful in troubleshooting a COM port problem.

For more information on this topic, see *A+ Exam Cram, 2ⁿᵈ Edition*, Chapter 9, the section "Serial (COM) Ports: 1 Bit after Another".

Question 26

The correct answer is a. Most modems use the Hayes Command set. This command set allows for standard communications between software and the modem. Some of the commands you will see are **ATH**, **ATZ**, and **ATDT**. The **ATH** command hangs up the modem from the telephone line. **ATZ** clears the modem and reinitializes it. The **ATDT** command is used to load the modem with a phone number to make an outbound call. Answers b and c are incorrect because Trivial File Transfer Protocol (TFTP) as well as File Transfer Protocol (FTP) are file transfer protocols used by computer networks. Answer d is incorrect; a Uniform Resource Locator (URL) is a site name in friendly format such as www.coriolis.com. This is used to access a Web site using a Web browser.

For more information on this topic, see *A+ Exam Cram, 2nd Edition*, Chapter 5, the section "Modems".

Question 27

The correct answer is d. A low-humidity/low-temperature environment is the most likely environment for Electro Static Discharge (ESD) conditions. If you are encountering static electricity discharges on door handles or such, you should be very cautious about ESD. Very small voltages can damage the components of most computer systems. Always remember to wear a ground strap if any possibility of ESD occurs. Answer a is incorrect because high humidity situations tend to minimize ESD effects. Answer b is incorrect because high temperature/high humidity situations prevent static buildup. High humidity usually prevents static electricity from building up, as does high temperature. Answer c is incorrect. High temperature situations tend to minimize static build-up in the air, minimizing ESD. The key to remember here is that low humidity is the most likely indicator of a static or ESD hazard being present. In some air-conditioned offices where moisture is controlled, a higher hazard exists for ESD than in normal atmospheric conditions.

For more information on this topic, see *A+ Exam Cram, 2nd Edition*, Chapter 5, the section "Basic Electronics".

Question 28

The correct answer is c. Ultra Wide SCSI allow for the connection of 15 additional devices to the chain. Remember that the SCSI controller will always require at least 1 address. Ultra Wide SCSI allows for a larger number of devices to be addressed than SCSI, which allows 8. Answers a and b are incorrect because Standard SCSI allows for the connection of 8 devices, or 7 not including the controller. Answer d is incorrect; at this time none of the SCSI interfaces support 32 devices.

For more information on this topic, see *A+ Exam Cram, 2nd Edition*, Chapter 8, the section "SCSI Interface".

Question 29

The correct answers are a and c. Each device on a SCSI chain requires a unique address. If a device in the middle of the chain has an internal terminator, it must be disabled because it will effectively terminate the chain and prevent access to the rest of the devices on the chain. The first and last devices on a SCSI chain terminate the entire bus. If these ends are not terminated, the entire chain will become unreliable. Answer b is incorrect because voltage is not relevant to a SCSI chain. Answer d is incorrect because NIC cards use a MAC address, not a SCSI device.

For more information on this topic, see *A+ Exam Cram, 2nd Edition*, Chapter 8, the section "SCSI Interface".

Question 30

The correct answer is b. Ink jet printers use a printer nozzle to spray the ink onto the paper. Answer a is incorrect because heat bonding is used by laser printers to melt toner onto the paper. Answer c is incorrect because *EP process* is the formal name of the laser printer process. Answer d is here to keep you on your toes and has no relationship to this question.

For more information on this topic, see *A+ Exam Cram, 2nd Edition*, Chapter 7, the section "Printers".

Question 31

The correct answer is a. Dots per inch (DPI) is the primary measurement of printer image quality in non-impact printers. Answer c is incorrect because Characters per inch (CPI) is the number of characters a printer can print in a single inch width. Answer d is incorrect because Lines per inch (LPI) is a measurement used to identify the number of lines that can be printed on a printer from a vertical perspective. Answer d is incorrect because RPI is not meaningful. Most laser printers offer DPI resolutions of 600, 1200, or above. Ink jet printers commonly offer at least 600 DPI resolution.

For more information on this topic, see *A+ Exam Cram, 2nd Edition*, Chapter 7, the section "Printers".

Question 32

The correct answer is c. By default, the first hard drive on a PC is reserved as drive C:. Answer a is incorrect because floppy disk drives are usually identified as A: or B:. Answer b is incorrect because CD-ROMs can use virtually any drive id, and the operating system will assign them the first available drive letter above drive C:. Answer d is incorrect for the same reason that answer c is incorrect. DVD drives also can be set to any valid location.

For more information on this topic, see *A+ Exam Cram, 2nd Edition*, Chapter 6, the section "Fixed Disks/Hard Drives".

Question 33

The correct answers are b and c. A CD-ROM can be read by a CD-ROM drive. DVD drives can also read CD-ROMs. Answers a and d are incorrect because the media is not compatible with these technologies.

For more information on this topic, see *A+ Exam Cram, 2nd Edition*, Chapter 6, the section "Optical Storage".

Question 34

The correct answer is b. The standard resolution for SVGA is 800×600. SVGA also supports 640×480, which is the standard resolution for VGA. Answer a is incorrect; the standard resolution for VGA is 640×480. Answer d is incorrect because the resolution of 512×1024 is not a standard resolution. Answer d is incorrect because the 1024×764 resolution is a very common resolution for flat panel and laptop computer systems but not the standard resolution for SVGA.

For more information on this topic, see *A+ Exam Cram, 2nd Edition*, Chapter 7, the section "SVGA and UVGA".

Question 35

The correct answer is d. If you attempt to force a disk controller cable onto the pins, you will potentially bend or break the connector. If the pins become broken, you can't replace them and must replace the drive. Answer a is incorrect because installing the control cable backward will only prevent the drive from working. Some control cables are keyed to prevent you from doing this, though it is still done quite often. Answer c is incorrect because the cable is keyed and cannot be physically installed upside down. Answer b is incorrect because configuring the master/slave jumper incorrectly will not damage the drive, but the drive may not function. You can have two slaves on the same bus, but not two masters. If you install the control cable backward, the drive will not operate but will not be damaged.

For more information on this topic, see *A+ Exam Cram, 2nd Edition*, Chapter 6, the section "Hard Drive Controllers".

Question 36

The correct answer is c. CD-ROMs can store between 650 and 700MB of data. Answer a is incorrect because 1.2MB is the standard storage for a high-density floppy drive. Answer b is incorrect because 360KB is the value of a low-density floppy drive. Answer d is incorrect because 5120MB is a number more in line with the storage capacity of a DVD.

For more information on this topic, see *A+ Exam Cram, 2nd Edition*, Chapter 6, the section "Optical Storage".

Question 37

The correct answer is c. The last device on a SCSI chain must be a terminator. Terminators come in one of two flavors: active or passive. Active terminators apply conditioning voltages to the line to keep things working properly. Passive terminators use resistive termination to keep the line terminated. Many SCSI devices have internal terminators that can be enabled to terminate the line. Answer a is incorrect because a truncator is not a device used in SCSI chains. Answer b is a data terminal device that is not relevant to SCSI devices; therefore, that answer is incorrect. Answer d is incorrect because you will not normally find a SCSI floppy drive; typically these drives will be using the integrated floppy controller on the motherboard.

For more information on this topic, see *A+ Exam Cram, 2nd Edition*, Chapter 8, the section "SCSI Interface".

Question 38

The correct answer is b. The **ATH** command will force a Hayes-compatible modem to disconnect from an active call. Answer a is incorrect because the **ATZ** command will cause the modem to reset to an initial state; this would include hanging up the line, but all internal settings will be reset to factory defaults when an **ATZ** command is accepted. Answer c is incorrect because the **ATDT** command is used to load a phone number for dial-out purposes. Answer d is incorrect because the **ATM** command is used to control speaker volume on a modem.

For more information on this topic, see *A+ Exam Cram, 2nd Edition*, Chapter 5, the section "Mice and Trackballs".

Question 39

The correct answer is a. The bus speed for the Pentium machine was 66MHz. Answer b is incorrect because the bus speed for the PCI bus by default was 33MHz. Answer c is incorrect because the 200 MHz speed refers to the internal bus speed for the processor. In the case of a Pentium 200, the internal bus speed is 200MHz. Answer d is incorrect because the Pentium II processor runs at a bus speed of either 100 or 133MHz. Pentium 4 processors run at a bus speed of 400MHz.

For more information on this topic, see *A+ Exam Cram, 2nd Edition*, Chapter 3, the section "Central Processing Unit (CPU)".

Question 40

The correct answer is d. If a normal startup occurred but no noise comes from the internal speaker, the speaker is either defective or has become disconnected. Answer a is incorrect because a video monitor failure would give you no indication of passing the POST or allow you to see the results of startup. Answer b is incorrect because a memory module failure would show itself during POST and give you a warning about memory failure. Answer d is incorrect because if the video adapter failed, the system would most likely not continue through boot up. A loose speaker wire is the most likely problem in this situation. The speaker should beep when the system is first turned on.

For more information on this topic, see *A+ Exam Cram, 2nd Edition*, Chapter 2, the section "Components of the Motherboard".

Question 41

The correct answers are a and b. The floppy or CD-ROM drive may have non-bootable disks in them. If they are higher in the boot order than the hard drive, the drive may not boot. First ensure that no floppy or CD-ROM media is in the unit. Next, you should check the boot sequence and verify that the hard drive is in the boot sequence. This is done at the SETUP level before the machine attempts to boot the operating system. Answer c is incorrect because a malfunctioning drive is a possible cause, but it would have a lower likelihood than the setup or non-bootable media. Answer d is incorrect; if the power supply malfunctioned, the system would probably not turn on or attempt a boot.

For more information on this topic, see *A+ Exam Cram, 2nd Edition*, Chapter 11, the section "Booting and System Files".

Question 42

The correct answer is a. When you get the "F1" message, you are being told that the BIOS has developed a setting error or has become corrupted for some reason. The most prudent thing to do at this point is to enter BIOS setup and reset the parameters to the default setting. Answer b is incorrect; a disk error may show itself during the boot up but will not usually wait for an F1 key to be depressed. Answer c is incorrect because normally if a video problem is detected during startup, it will give you a definitive error message and code. Answer d is incorrect; memory problems will give you an error message and then prompt for input (sometimes with the F1 key).

For more information on this topic, see *A+ Exam Cram, 2nd Edition*, Chapter 11, the section "Booting and System Files".

Question 43

The correct answer is b. The "dreaded 301" error probably means that either a key on the keyboard is stuck, the keyboard has failed, or that the keyboard connector has come loose from the back panel. You may get a 301 error if you leave something laying on a key when you start up the computer. Answer a is incorrect because memory problems manifest themselves during the memory check of the POST process with other error message numbers. Answer c is incorrect because the video systems have another set of error numbers. Answer d is incorrect because multimedia circuitry is not normally tested at the POST level but at the operating systems level.

For more information on this topic, see *A+ Exam Cram, 2nd Edition*, Chapter 4, the section "Read-Only Memory (ROM)".

Question 44

The correct answer is a. The network card and printer port may be sharing the same IRQ address. Answer b is incorrect because MAC addresses are established by the network card manufacturer and should only be relevant to networking addresses. Answer c is incorrect because a defective video card would not cause network or intermittent printer problems. Answer d is incorrect because memory problems are usually detected during boot up.

For more information on this topic, see *A+ Exam Cram, 2nd Edition*, Chapter 8, the section "Networking Overview".

Question 45

The correct answer is a. A USB Hub allows for the connection of additional USB devices. Hubs come in a variety of sizes: anywhere from 2 to 16 connections. Answer b is incorrect because a post box is not a computer term. Answer c is incorrect because a router is a device used to send messages across a network and would not normally be connected to a USB port. Answer d is incorrect because terminators are used in SCSI and coaxial-based networks to ensure that both ends of the cable are properly conditioned and electrically terminated.

For more information on this topic, see *A+ Exam Cram, 2nd Edition*, Chapter 8, the section "Universal Serial Bus (USB)".

Question 46

The correct answer is a. The first thing that occurs after the PC is turned on is that a signal called "voltage good" is generated. The voltage good signal causes the CPU or microprocessor to begin running the POST process. The POST process on Intel-based processors always has the same address, which is contained in the system ROM. Answer b is incorrect because an Initial Program Load (IPL) is the first step in loading the operating system once the POST has been passed. Answer c is incorrect because interrupts are loaded during the boot process. Answer d is incorrect because plug-and-play configuration is also established during the boot process after the BIOS is loaded.

For more information on this topic, see *A+ Exam Cram, 2nd Edition*, Chapter 4, the section "Read-Only Memory (ROM)".

Question 47

The correct answer is b. 10BaseT requires a cable capable of a minimum of 10Mbps data rate. The lowest assurance of proper bandwidth is the CAT 3 cable. Answer a is incorrect because CAT 5 cables are certified at 100Mbps. Answer c is incorrect because CAT 1 cables are generally unsuitable for networking. Answer d is incorrect because fiber-optic cables are not compatible with 10BaseT networks.

For more information on this topic, see *A+ Exam Cram, 2nd Edition*, Chapter 9, the section "Network Cables and Connectors".

Question 48

The correct answer is d. Many older computer systems only had one IDE controller. These controllers could have a maximum of two devices attached to them. In order to add a second controller, you would need to add an expansion card. (These cards are usually very inexpensive.) Most of these cards were only available on ISA-type expansion slots. All new PC systems include two integrated IDE controllers on the motherboard for a capability of four drives. If you need to go beyond four drives, you can still buy IDE controllers, but I would strongly suggest you investigate SCSI devices at that point. Answer a is incorrect because the cables and controller standards are incompatible. Answer b is incorrect for the reasons explained for the correct answer, d. Answer c is incorrect because you have a limit of two devices per controller on IDE interfaces.

For more information on this topic, see *A+ Exam Cram, 2nd Edition*, Chapter 5, the section "IRQs, DMA, and I/O Ports".

Question 49

The correct answer is c. Each IDE channel can support two physical drives. The first drive on each channel will probably already be configured as a master. You cannot have two masters on the same channel. You can however have two slaves on the same channel. By convention, the device with the highest performance requirements will be configured as a master, the second device as a slave. Answer a is incorrect because of the potential of having two masters on a single channel. Answer b is incorrect for the same reason that answer a is incorrect. Answer d is incorrect because the controllers and cabling is incompatible.

For more information on this topic, see *A+ Exam Cram, 2nd Edition*, Chapter 5, the section "IRQs, DMA, and I/O Ports".

Question 50

The correct answer is a. The CMOS stores system parameters during power off. The battery on the motherboard powers the CMOS during system-off states. Answer b is incorrect because read-only memory (ROM) cannot be updated to store settings except in special circumstances. Answer c is incorrect because RAM looses its memory when the power is turned off. Obviously answer d is here just to see if you're on your toes.

For more information on this topic, see *A+ Exam Cram, 2nd Edition*, Chapter 4, the section "Read-Only Memory (ROM)".

Question 51

The correct answer is d. Video connectors are typically 15-pin connectors called DB-15 type. Answer a is incorrect because connector A is a USB port and will not accept a video monitor directly. Answer b is incorrect because connector B is a 36-pin Centronics parallel printer port. Answer c is incorrect because connector C is a DB-25 printer port connection.

For more information on this topic, see *A+ Exam Cram, 2ⁿᵈ Edition*, Chapter 9, the section "Parallel (LPT) Ports: 8 Bits Across".

Question 52

The correct answer is b. The type of RAM used for caching is static RAM (SRAM). SRAM is very fast and does not need periodic refreshing. This means that the processor will not have to wait if the memory is being refreshed. Answer a is incorrect because VRAM is the type of memory used in video cards. Answer c is incorrect because DRAM is most frequently used for main memory and is usually slower than SRAM. Answer d is incorrect because CMOS is considered read-only memory and would not be able to store information that requires frequent updates.

For more information on this topic, see *A+ Exam Cram, 2ⁿᵈ Edition*, Chapter 3, the section "L-1 and L-2 Caches".

Question 53

The correct answers are a and b. Cache that is built into the microprocessor is referred to as Level 1 (L1) cache. Caching that sits on the motherboard is called Level 2 (L2) cache. L1 cache is the fastest RAM memory on the system, though it is usually very small in amount in comparison to the other memory on the system. L2 cache typically runs from 64KB to 1MB. L2 cache is also very fast, as is SRAM. Answers c and d are incorrect because they do not refer to caching memory used on PC systems.

For more information on this topic, see *A+ Exam Cram, 2ⁿᵈ Edition*, Chapter 3, the section "L-1 and L-2 Caches".

Question 54

The correct answer is b. The 1701 error is a standard for indicating a hard drive controller failure. If this shows up during startup, you probably have a defective integrated controller on the motherboard. You can frequently replace an integrated controller with a controller for the PCI or ISA bus (ISA is not recommended). Answer a is incorrect; the standard error for a keyboard is 301. Answer c is incorrect because a CPU failure will frequently not start or pass the POST test. Answer d is incorrect because NMI circuitry on the CPU is tested as part of the CPU diagnostics.

For more information on this topic, see *A+ Exam Cram, 2nd Edition*, Chapter 4, the section "Read-Only Memory (ROM)".

Question 55

The correct answer is a. System units and monitors can accumulate a great deal of dust over time. This dust can clog air filters as well as insulate integrated circuits from good airflow. The internal operating temperature of the Integrated Circuits (ICs) will often exceed design parameters and fail prematurely. It is a good idea, depending on the environment, to remove dust from system units on a regular basis (I recommend quarterly). Monitors also tend to attract dust due to the high voltage they generate. Again, heat will cause the premature failure of components. Answer b is incorrect because Electro Static Discharge (ESD) is not a function of dust, although static electricity attracts dust particles. Answer c is incorrect because I/O channel clatter is just an invented term for this question. Answer d is currently incorrect. On early computer systems, dust was the enemy of hard disk drives. Today, virtually all hard drives are sealed units that dust is not able to enter. However, a speck of dust the width of a human hair can cause permanent damage to a hard drive if it were allowed to contaminate the drive surface.

For more information on this topic, see *A+ Exam Cram, 2nd Edition*, Chapter 6, the section "Fixed Disks/Hard Drives".

Question 56

The correct answer is b. If you come upon a system that is working after boards have been removed, you can pretty well establish that either a hardware malfunction has occurred or that a resource error is occurring (such as IRQ conflicts). Work from what works and install the boards one at a time to determine if a malfunction is occurring. Answer a may work as well, but is not as good an answer as b. Answer a will probably take you longer to troubleshoot than taking the task on one board at a time. Answer c is always worth a try, but if the system is torn apart already, why make someone put it back together and take it apart again? Answer d is incorrect: Depending on the situation, you may want to notify your supervisor, but I'd do that after I restored the system to operation or diagnosed the problem.

For more information on this topic, see *A+ Exam Cram, 2nd Edition*, Chapter 14, the section "Hardware Problems".

Question 57

The correct answer is b. If the control cable on a floppy disk is installed backward, the drive will show activity—spin continuously but not load or boot. This is a sure sign that the cable is backward. Answer a is possible but not as likely as b. A floppy disk malfunction may have occurred, but first check the cable. Answer c is incorrect; the IDE controller has nothing to do with the floppy disk and will identify itself as a potential problem later. Answer d is incorrect because you do not know if the new hard drive is defective until you repair the floppy disk problem.

For more information on this topic, see *A+ Exam Cram, 2nd Edition*, Chapter 14, the section "Hardware Problems".

Question 58

The correct answer is b. A gateway converts protocols from one environment to another. You would potentially use a gateway if you were trying to connect from TCP/IP to NetWare in a local area network. Answer a is incorrect; a router is used to break a large network into smaller networks. Routers are used when you want to connect an office network to the Internet. A router contains software that also stores information about how to contact remote systems. Answer c is incorrect because you will encounter hubs in one of two environments: a local area network, where systems are connected to each other in a star configuration (usually), and in working with USB devices. USB hubs allow the connection of multiple USB devices to a single USB port. Answer d is incorrect; a bypass connector is something that can be used to bypass an electrical connection and has nothing to do with protocol conversion.

For more information on this topic, see *A+ Exam Cram, 2nd Edition*, Chapter 8, the section "Bridges and Routers".

Question 59

The correct answers are a, c, and d. Answer b is incorrect because in all probability, if the system is booting fine off a CD-ROM or floppy, then the power supply is working correctly. You will probably need to open the case and check all the connections to the hard drives. Over time, the power cables may come loose, the control cable may have been switched, or a jumper may have been set. In troubleshooting a system with this type of problem, do not assume that the user who called you knows anything about what happened to the system. Repeatedly, people have tried to upgrade systems and encountered a difficulty and may be reluctant to be honest with you about what they have done. A good rule of thumb in these situations is to make no assumptions about what is wrong.

For more information on this topic, see *A+ Exam Cram, 2nd Edition*, Chapter 14, the section "Hardware Problems".

Question 60

The correct answer is d. Video monitors usually use a 15-pin connector. Answer a is incorrect because serial ports typically use a 9-pin connection. Answer b is incorrect because printer ports on the back of a PC use a 25-pin connection. Answer c is incorrect because the USB port is a small connector, and it uses a special USB connector.

For more information on this topic, see *A+ Exam Cram, 2nd Edition*, Chapter 2, the section "Components of the Motherboard".

Question 61

The correct answers are a and b. SCSI chains require that the both ends be terminated. The SCSI controller, which is at the beginning of the chain, serves as a terminator. The last device in a chain will not serve as a terminator unless the device has an internal terminator and it is enabled. Most SCSI devices have two ports on them: an input and an output. The input is closest to the controller, and the output goes to the next device in the chain or the terminator. Answer c is incorrect because a terminator in the middle of the chain would disable the devices after it. Answer d is incorrect because SCSI requires termination on both ends of the chain.

For more information on this topic, see *A+ Exam Cram, 2nd Edition*, Chapter 8, the section "SCSI Interface".

Question 62

The correct answer is b. One of the nice things about USB is the ability to hot plug devices into the port. The operating system will typically automatically run an install wizard (if Microsoft) and ask for configuration drivers or use internal ones if available. Answer a is incorrect; you do not have to power a system down in order to install or remove a USB device, except when told to do so by the manufacturer. Answer c is incorrect. You won't need to reset the BIOS because the USB connection is managed by the operating system. Answer d is incorrect; you should not have to reformat a hard drive to add a USB device.

For more information on this topic, see *A+ Exam Cram, 2nd Edition*, Chapter 8, the section "Universal Serial Bus (USB)".

Question 63

The correct answers are a and d. A serial mouse can be connected to one of your COM ports. You will need to install a serial mouse driver and configure the port properly for it to work. It is also highly recommended that you power down the system when installing a mouse on the computer. (Always follow available manufacturer instructions, and if in doubt, powering down the system will do no harm.) Answer b is incorrect; many systems will let you have a PS/2 and serial mouse together. Both will work as if they were separate. Answer c is incorrect; if you use a COM port for your mouse—say COM1—you should not use COM3 for anything. You will have intermittent problems with your mouse or the other COM device if you do that.

For more information on this topic, see *A+ Exam Cram, 2nd Edition*, Chapter 5, the section "Mice and Trackballs".

Question 64

The correct answer is a. Most systems will issue one short beep when POST is completed. Usually anything other than one beep is an indication of a problem with the system. Answer b is incorrect. On most systems, two beeps indicate that you have a memory parity problem. Answer c is incorrect; three beeps indicates a memory failure. Answer d is incorrect; four beeps indicates that the system timer is not working on many systems. Beep codes are very vendor specific, and you would want to go to the BIOS provider's Web site and get the beep code information for the BIOS you are using.

For more information on this topic, see *A+ Exam Cram, 2nd Edition*, Chapter 11, the section "Beep Codes".

Question 65

The correct answer is b, false. A PC Card allows for hot swapping of cards, which makes changing configurations very easy. When a new card is first installed, you will need to install drivers and configure them correctly. After that, you can swap out cards and install other cards, and the system will reconfigure appropriately.

For more information on this topic, see *A+ Exam Cram, 2ⁿᵈ Edition*, Chapter 2, the section "PC Card (PCMCIA)".

Question 66

The correct answer is b. It is very critical that a BIOS upgrade not be interrupted in the middle. Answer a is incorrect; many IBM portables will test for battery operation and not allow a BIOS upgrade unless the system is running on a power supply. If a BIOS upgrade is interrupted, in some systems, the only way to repair them is to replace the motherboard (this is very typical for laptop systems). Follow the upgrade instructions to the letter. Answer c is incorrect; when you perform an upgrade, the BIOS will in most cases be set to a default setting by the upgrade BIOS's upgrade program. Answer d is incorrect; you should never disconnect the CMOS battery unless directed by the manufacturer because you will lose all settings.

For more information on this topic, see *A+ Exam Cram, 2ⁿᵈ Edition*, Chapter 4, the section "Read-Only Memory (ROM)".

Question 67

The correct answer is a. The first thing that occurs in a cold boot is a POST test. A warm boot, such as a Ctrl+Alt+Del performs a warm boot and bypasses the POST. Answer b is incorrect; an IPL occurs when the system is ready to boot the operating system. Answer c is incorrect; the operating system is loaded during the IPL process. Answer d is incorrect. NMI configurations are not a consideration in this situation.

For more information on this topic, see *A+ Exam Cram, 2ⁿᵈ Edition*, Chapter 4, the section "Memory Diagnostics—Parity".

Question 68

The correct answer is b. Multimedia cards, like all expansion cards, minimally require that the IRQ, DMA, and I/O addresses be set properly. In plug-and-play systems, this is done automatically as part of the installation process. In older or legacy systems, you may have to set jumpers on the board to have it operate correctly. Answer a is incorrect because the manufacturer of a network card assigns the MAC address you are using. Each MAC address is unique in the entire world (supposedly). Answers c and d are incorrect because Himem settings are the set when the operating system loads and should not be a factor in this instance.

For more information on this topic, see *A+ Exam Cram, 2ⁿᵈ Edition*, Chapter 5, the section "IRQs, DMA, and I/O Ports".

Question 69

The correct answers are a and b. The POST will normally pause at an error to give you time to evaluate what has failed. The 1701 followed by "Press F1 to continue" message will wait for the F1 key on the keyboard to be depressed. The 1701 message indicates a disk controller error. Some versions will also give you a text message such as a disk controller error, some do not. The POST will continue either to completion or to the next error, where you will get another F1 pause. Answer c is incorrect because the F1 request will occur after an error message about the video system has occurred. Answer d is incorrect because the POST process first checks the memory for proper operation.

For more information on this topic, see *A+ Exam Cram, 2nd Edition*, Chapter 11, the section "Booting and System files".

Question 70

The correct answer is c. If the error goes away when you remove the board, it may be as a result of a hardware malfunction, or a resource conflict such as IRQ. Answer a is incorrect. If the system is working properly without the card installed, you might want to verify whether the power supply is being overloaded and shutting down, but more likely the problem is a resource or card malfunction. Answer b is incorrect; the floppy drive should have nothing to do with the expansion card. Answer d is incorrect; if the motherboard is malfunctioning, you will probably notice other problems.

For more information on this topic, see *A+ Exam Cram, 2nd Edition*, Chapter 14, the section "Hardware Problems".

A+ Core Hardware Practice Test #2

Question 1

What is the typical form factor for a desktop machine?

- ○ a. ATX
- ○ b. AT
- ○ c. DAT
- ○ d. FAT

Question 2

You are trying to install a second hard drive onto an IDE channel on the motherboard. The first channel already has a hard drive and a CD-ROM configured and is working properly. How would you configure this drive on the second channel?

- ○ a. Configure the drive as a master on the second channel.
- ○ b. Attach the drive to a SCSI controller and reconfigure it appropriately.
- ○ c. Change the power supply jumpers to accept secondary power.
- ○ d. Reverse the cable on the master controller and install the drive.

Question 3

You have just installed a 1000MHz Pentium processor. When you boot up
this system, you are only seeing the speed of the 400MHz chip that was
previously installed. What is the likely problem?

○ a. You cannot install a 1000MHz chip onto a 400MHz motherboard.

○ b. The BIOS has not been updated to 1000MHz support.

○ c. The Firmware definitely needs to be upgraded.

○ d. The Pentium chip has malfunctioned.

Question 4

Your system periodically reboots for no apparent reason after you installed
a new sound card. What is a likely problem in this situation?

○ a. The BIOS does not support this sound card.

○ b. The IRQ address is set incorrectly.

○ c. The power supply is overloaded.

○ d. The processor intermix ratio is set incorrectly.

Question 5

Which of the following is probably the most cost effective solution if the
integrated IDE controller on the motherboard fails?

○ a. Replace the motherboard.

○ b. Install a new IDE controller into an expansion port.

○ c. Reformat the hard drive to NTFS.

○ d. Cross jumper the working IDE controller to support four drives.

Question 6

When you install a new plug-and-play card into your system, what will the BIOS do?

○ a. Require you to manually set the parameters of the card.

○ b. Read the ECSD to determine what resources are available and are needed by the card.

○ c. Configure the MAC address for the card for proper operation.

○ d. Set the NMI for 0HEF to configure the card for Initial Program Load.

Question 7

Which of the following SCSI ID numbers has the highest priority?

○ a. 8

○ b. 5

○ c. 0

○ d. 16

Question 8

You want to upgrade the video adapter on a desktop PC. The desktop PC is very new. Which slot would be optimum for a new video card?

○ a. PCI

○ b. AGP

○ c. IDE

○ d. ISA

Question 9

You have been asked to troubleshoot a system that has been turned off for some time. The customer indicates that the date information is not being kept from day to day. Each time they reboot the system, the date and time are not correct. What is the most likely suspect?

○ a. The BIOS is out of date and needs to be upgraded.

○ b. The plug-and-play mapper has malfunctioned.

○ c. The battery on the motherboard is dead.

○ d. The operating system needs to be refreshed from original distribution.

Question 10

The system you are troubleshooting passes POST most of the time. You notice that it passes POST when the machine has been turned off for a while. However, when it has been running for about an hour the POST test fails at the memory test. What is the most likely problem?

○ a. The BIOS refresh rate is set incorrectly.

○ b. A memory chip has a heat problem.

○ c. The CPU chip has a heat problem.

○ d. This is normal operation for most modern PCs.

Question 11

The DB-15 male connector is used for:

○ a. Video monitor

○ b. Parallel port

○ c. USB port

○ d. Serial port

Question 12

What is the standard type of keyboard connector for an AT or ATX motherboard?

○ a. 6-pin PS/2

○ b. DB-9 round

○ c. DB-15 flat

○ d. 5-pin Molex

Question 13

The time is takes for a CRT's electron beam to travel from the top of the screen to the bottom is called the:

○ a. Synch Rate

○ b. Refresh Rate

○ c. Masking Rate

○ d. Frequency

Question 14

The IDE primary controller address uses which default I/O address?

○ a. 1F0H

○ b. 2H0F

○ c. 1H0F

○ d. 3BEF

Question 15

Analog modems use which type of connection for the phone line?

○ a. RJ-11

○ b. RJ-45

○ c. DB-15

○ d. DB-25

Question 16

What is the Hayes compatible command to reset your modem?

○ a. **ATH**

○ b. **ATZ**

○ c. **ATDT**

○ d. **+++**

Question 17

You want to install three USB devices on your computer. Your computer only has two USB connectors. What must be done to install the third device?

○ a. You can connect only two USB devices to a computer system.

○ b. Add a hub to one of the USB ports and install two USB devices onto the hub.

○ c. Cross jumper the hub to bypass the USB limit interlock.

○ d. Upgrade to IEEE 1394 to avoid this problem.

Question 18

A UPS protects a computer system from which type of problem?

○ a. EDI

○ b. ESD

○ c. Power surges

○ d. EMI

Question 19

You boot up a system and receive a 301 POST error. What does this indicate?

○ a. Memory failure

○ b. Power supply failure

○ c. Keyboard error

○ d. Floppy drive error

Question 20

> You want to install an additional USB device on your system. Which of the following is true?
>
> ○ a. You can plug it in with the computer running.
>
> ○ b. You must power the computer down to install a device.
>
> ○ c. You must reset the BIOS for this device to work properly.
>
> ○ d. You can plug it in, but it will not work until the computer is rebooted.

Question 21

> You are printing a report on a dot-matrix printer. The print quality has suddenly become very poor and you notice fuzz on the paper. What needs to be done to correct this problem?
>
> ○ a. Replace the printer ribbon and clean the print head.
>
> ○ b. Only replace the printer ribbon.
>
> ○ c. Change to a different type of paper; the bond weight is improper for a dot-matrix printer.
>
> ○ d. Replace the print head because it has malfunctioned.

Question 22

> Which of the following parallel ports standards has the highest throughput?
>
> ○ a. SPP
>
> ○ b. ECP
>
> ○ c. EPP
>
> ○ d. BSDI

Question 23

You want to install a 100BaseT network in your office. What is the minimum cable specification that should be used?

○ a. CAT 1

○ b. CAT 3

○ c. CAT 5

○ d. CAT 10

Question 24

The maximum cable length for a 10BaseT network is:

○ a. 50 meters

○ b. 100 meters

○ c. 200 meters

○ d. 385 meters

Question 25

A 10Base2 based network uses which topology?

○ a. Bus

○ b. Star

○ c. Ring

○ d. Mesh

Question 26

A 10BaseT based network uses which topology?

○ a. Bus

○ b. Star

○ c. Ring

○ d. Mesh

Question 27

How many devices can be connected to a Fast/Wide SCSI-2 bus?

○ a. 8

○ b. 15

○ c. 16

○ d. 31

Question 28

What is the memory contained inside the CPU called?

○ a. L1 cache

○ b. L ll cache

○ c. L lll cache

○ d. Hash cache

Question 29

What is the default IRQ for COM2?

○ a. IRQ 2

○ b. IRQ 3

○ c. IRQ 4

○ d. IRQ 1

Question 30

A two-way connection that can communicate in only one direction at a time is called:

○ a. Full-duplex

○ b. Asynchronous

○ c. Half-duplex

○ d. Bisynchronous

Question 31

You have just installed a new hard drive on your computer. When you try to format this drive you get the following message: "Invalid media type." What should you do to fix this problem?

○ a. The hard drive is defective and should be replaced.

○ b. Run FDISK and partition the drive.

○ c. Run CHKDSK to fix the MBR for the drive.

○ d. Run SCANDISK and do a surface analysis.

Question 32

You have made a boot floppy. When you start your system, however, the hard drive boots up. You want to boot from the floppy disk to install an upgrade. What should you do to fix this problem?

○ a. Run **Format** on the hard drive to initialize the disk.

○ b. Run **Format** on the floppy to initialize the floppy.

○ c. Check the boot sequence on the BIOS after the system has loaded to change boot order.

○ d. Check the boot sequence on the BIOS during setup to change boot order.

Question 33

You have been asked to install an additional hard drive on an older system. Upon inspection of the system, you only find one IDE connector on the motherboard. What must you do to install this drive?

○ a. You cannot install this drive; you must replace the motherboard.

○ b. Obtain an additional IDE controller for an expansion port and install the drive on that port.

○ c. Obtain a three-connector IDE cable and install the drive on the existing controller.

○ d. Attach the drive to the floppy cable and reconfigure the BIOS.

Question 34

A computer user has called you and indicated that a system will not boot up. The system was previously working fine and nothing has changed in the configuration. The POST is working correctly and giving no indications of a malfunction. What would be one of the first things you should check with the user?

○ a. That the system is plugged in.

○ b. That the hard drive is correctly formatted.

○ c. That the floppy disk drive does not contain a disk.

○ d. That the CD-ROM has been unmounted.

Question 35

You have just received a call from a customer who indicates that a computer system is not powering on properly. All cables appear to be plugged in correctly. What should you do to verify operational status of the equipment? [Choose the three best answers]

❑ a. Have the customer plug a different device into the wall socket.

❑ b. Verify that the electrical connections are good.

❑ c. Verify that the power switch is turned on.

❑ d. Replace the power supply.

Question 36

Which of the following processor types will work in a slot 1 socket? [Choose the three best answers]

❑ a. Pentium II

❑ b. Pentium III

❑ c. Celeron

❑ d. Pentium III Xeon

Question 37

What is a battery backup also known as?

○ a. UPS

○ b. Surge suppresser

○ c. Voltage regulator

○ d. ESD eliminator

Question 38

ISA cards have which bus data width?

○ a. 8-16 bits

○ b. 16-32 bits

○ c. 8-16-32 bits

○ d. 64 bits

Question 39

You want to upgrade the memory on a motherboard. You observe the memory on the motherboard is 168-pin DIMM. How many DIMMs are required for each memory bank?

○ a. 1

○ b. 2

○ c. 3

○ d. 4

Question 40

You want to ensure that your hard drives are operating at peak speed. What should you do to improve performance?

○ a. Run **FDISK** on a regular basis to optimize disk storage.

○ b. Run a defrag program to organize disk files.

○ c. Run a disk compression program to organize data.

○ d. Run **Format** to improve FAT entries.

Question 41

You have just moved a computer system to a new office. When you turn on the computer and monitor, you notice that the monitor intermittently changes colors or backgrounds. What is the most likely problem?

○ a. Loose video adapter

○ b. Defective monitor

○ c. Loose video cable

○ d. Power sags on the new electrical connection

Question 42

What is the I/O address of LPT2?

○ a. 03E8

○ b. 02E8

○ c. 0278

○ d. 0378

Question 43

You have just purchased a new UPS and want to install it on your computer server. Which devices should not be connected to your UPS in order to ensure maximum battery life? [Choose the three best answers]

❑ a. Laser printer

❑ b. Monitor

❑ c. Keyboard

❑ d. Electrically amplified speakers

Question 44

You want to buy a fire extinguisher for your office in the event of a computer fire. Which type of extinguisher should you buy?

○ a. Class A

○ b. Class B

○ c. Class C

○ d. Class D

Question 45

Which expansion bus should not be used on a modern PC system? [Choose the two best answers]

❑ a. ISA

❑ b. EISA

❑ c. PCI

❑ d. USB

Question 46

Your AT class computer has how many DMA channels?

○ a. 2

○ b. 4

○ c. 8

○ d. DMA has been eliminated from AT class computers.

Question 47

You have a PC portable computer. You are going to add a Type 3 PC Card to it. How many Type 3 cards can a standard portable accept?

○ a. 1

○ b. 2

○ c. 3

○ d. 4

Question 48

The USB port uses how many IRQs?

○ a. 1

○ b. 2

○ c. 3

○ d. 4

Question 49

USB offers which of the following advantages? [Choose the three best answers]

❑ a. Easy to configure

❑ b. High speed data processing

❑ c. Power on replacement

❑ d. Fault tolerant redundancy

Question 50

Which of the following types of devices can be installed on a USB port? [Choose the three best answers]

❑ a. Digital camera

❑ b. Printer

❑ c. SCSI disk

❑ d. Expansion memory

Question 51

What type of devices does SCSI normally support? [Choose the two best answers]

❑ a. Modem

❑ b. Printer

❑ c. Scanner

❑ d. Hard drive

Question 52

A USB port can support how many devices?

○ a. 16

○ b. 32

○ c. 127

○ d. 255

Question 53

You want to send a message from one PDA to another. Which method would be most likely used?

- ○ a. IR
- ○ b. USB
- ○ c. LAN
- ○ d. FTP

Question 54

You want to install additional memory on a system that supports both DIMM and SIMM memory. You notice the DIMM slots are full, but the SIMM slots are not. You install additional memory in the SIMM slots. The computer boots but will not recognize the additional memory. What is the most likely problem?

- ○ a. A bad memory module.
- ○ b. Power supply problems.
- ○ c. Memory conflicts in the bank switches.
- ○ d. The motherboard does not support both memory types simultaneously.

Question 55

What is the data bus width for a PCI slot?

- ○ a. 8
- ○ b. 16
- ○ c. 32
- ○ d. 64

Question 56

SDRAM memory has which of the following capabilities? [Choose the two best answers]

❑ a. High speed burst data transfer

❑ b. Static memory

❑ c. Nonvolatile memory capability

❑ d. Dynamic refresh

Question 57

Users report that a 10Base2 network does not appear to be functioning. Shares and printers are no longer accessible. Which of the following are likely causes of the problem?

○ a. The hub has malfunctioned.

○ b. A terminator has malfunctioned.

○ c. The power supply for the network is defective.

○ d. A server has malfunctioned and has gone offline.

Question 58

Toner is melted onto the paper in a laser printer at which stage of the printing process?

○ a. Charging

○ b. Fusing

○ c. Discharging

○ d. Transfer

Question 59

You want to connect two computers together in a 10BaseT network. Which type of cable should you use?

○ a. CAT 5 crossover cable

○ b. CAT 5 normal cable

○ c. RS232 null modem cable

○ d. IEEE 4888 high-speed data cable

Question 60

Your dot-matrix printer is only printing half the characters on each line. What is the likely problem?

○ a. Defective print head

○ b. Paper misalignment

○ c. Platen misalignment

○ d. Paper limiting switch malfunction

Question 61

A Windows network that is a peer-to-peer type is referred to by which name?

○ a. Domain base

○ b. Client-Server network

○ c. Workgroup

○ d. 10BaseT

Question 62

MMX technology was added to Pentium processor for which purpose?

○ a. Faster overall processor performance

○ b. Multimedia and video performance improvements

○ c. Math and computational speed

○ d. Floating-point arithmetic

Question 63

A dot-matrix printer typically uses which type of paper feed?

○ a. Pressure feed

○ b. Vacuum feed

○ c. Tractor feed

○ d. Gravity feed

Question 64

The output of your laser printer is completely black. What is the most likely problem with the printer?

○ a. Fusing unit malfunction

○ b. Static discharge malfunction

○ c. Clogged scavenger bar

○ d. Defective control unit

Question 65

WRAM is used for which function?

○ a. Video memory

○ b. Cache memory

○ c. DIMM expansion memory

○ d. PCI bus accelerator memory

Question 66

Dot-matrix printers use which measurement for speed? [Choose the two best answers]

❑ a. CPS

❑ b. PPM

❑ c. LPM

❑ d. CPM

Question 67

The 10/100 on a NIC card refers to which parameter?

- ○ a. Minimum/Maximum cable length
- ○ b. Megabits per second
- ○ c. Megabytes per second
- ○ d. IRQ/DMA pairing

Question 68

You want to attach your new NIC card to your network. You notice that the card has an RJ-45 connector on the back. What is the most likely network topology in use? [Choose the two best answers]

- ❏ a. 10BaseT
- ❏ b. 100BaseT
- ❏ c. 10Base2
- ❏ d. 1Base10

Question 69

A power supply capacity is typically measured by which term?

- ○ a. Wattage
- ○ b. Voltage
- ○ c. Amperage
- ○ d. Resistance

Question 70

You are replacing COM3 with a modem. What I/O address should the modem be normally configured for?

- ○ a. 03E8H
- ○ b. 02E8H
- ○ c. 03EF8
- ○ d. 02EF8

4

A+ Core Hardware
Answer Key #2

1. a	19. c	37. a	55. c
2. a	20. a	38. a	56. a, d
3. b	21. a	39. a	57. b
4. b	22. b	40. b	58. b
5. b	23. c	41. c	59. a
6. b	24. b	42. c	60. c
7. b	25. a	43. a, b, d	61. c
8. b	26. b	44. c	62. b
9. c	27. b	45. a, b	63. c
10. b	28. a	46. c	64. d
11. a	29. b	47. a	65. a
12. a	30. c	48. a	66. a, c
13. b	31. b	49. a, b, c	67. b
14. a	32. d	50. a, b, d	68. a, b
15. a	33. b	51. c, d	69. a
16. b	34. c	52. c	70. a
17. b	35. a, b, c	53. a	
18. c	36. a, b, c	54. d	

Question 1

The correct answer is a. Virtually all modern desktop PC systems use the ATX form factor motherboard. The ATX form has most of the connectors already installed for the COM and LPT ports. Answer b is incorrect because the AT form factor is an older motherboard style. The AT form factor requires all the connectors to be installed on the motherboard and then physically bolted onto the case. Answer c is incorrect; DAT is a digital magnetic tape format. Answer d is incorrect; FAT is a file system used in Windows-based operating systems.

For more information on this topic, see *A+ Exam Cram, 2nd Edition*, Chapter 2, the section "Components of the Motherboard".

Question 2

The correct answer is a. You would attach this drive onto the second channel of the system as the master. The first device attached on an IDE should be configured as the master drive. The second drive on the same IDE channel would be configured as a slave. Answer b is incorrect because IDE drives are not compatible with SCSI drives. Answer c is incorrect; power jumpers do not affect the installation of the hard drives. Answer d is incorrect because cable reversal will not add this drive as a master.

For more information on this topic, see *A+ Exam Cram, 2nd Edition*, Chapter 14, the section "Hardware Problems".

Question 3

The correct answer is b. Many motherboards were designed before the 1000MHz chip was manufactured. Generally, you can run a motherboard BIOS upgrade to support the faster chips, though older motherboards may not accept this speed processor even with a BIOS upgrade. Answer a is incorrect; if the board does not support upgrades to the faster chip, it may still run the chip at the fastest rate supported by the motherboard. Answer c is incorrect; you should check the manufacturer's support documentation to see what is the fastest speed the motherboard will support. The firmware may need to be upgraded, but that will not be established until the documentation has been reviewed. Answer d is incorrect; no indication of a malfunction of the chip is indicated by the symptom.

For more information on this topic, see *A+ Exam Cram, 2nd Edition*, Chapter 3, the section "Central Processing Unit (CPU)".

Question 4

The correct answer is b. An IRQ problem may cause a system to lock up or periodically reboot. You should check for IRQ or other resource conflicts before deciding the board is bad. Answer a is incorrect; the BIOS not supporting a sound card is irrelevant. BIOS settings do not generally affect device installation. Answer c is incorrect; the power supply is probably not overloaded but this is less likely than a resource conflict. Answer d is incorrect; there is no such thing as a processor intermix setting except on Star Trek.

For more information on this topic, see *A+ Exam Cram, 2nd Edition*, Chapter 5, the section "Interrupt Requests (IRQs)".

Question 5

The correct answer is b. Generally you can install an IDE controller into either an ISA or PCI slot to replace an on-board controller. You may need to reconfigure the BIOS for this to operate. Answer a is incorrect; you may want to replace the motherboard when time permits, but it is not necessary in most cases until it is time to upgrade. Answer c is incorrect; reformatting a hard drive would not solve a controller failure. Answer d is incorrect because you cannot cross jumper an IDE controller. IDE controllers can only control two devices. The key to this question is the fact that the most cost-effective solution was asked for. An add-in controller will almost always cost less than replacing the motherboard.

For more information on this topic, see *A+ Exam Cram, 2nd Edition*, Chapter 9, the section "Basic I/O Interfaces".

Question 6

The correct answer is b. One of the steps of BIOS loading is to scan the Extended System Configuration Data (ESCD) storage area to determine what plug-and-play resources are needed. Each time the system is booted or shut down, the ESCD data area is updated. Answer a is incorrect; you do not need to manually configure parameters on a plug-and-play card. This defeats the purpose of plug-and-play. Answer c is incorrect; MAC addresses are used in the physical network connection and have nothing to do with the ESCD or BIOS. Answer d is incorrect; non-maskable interrupt (NMI) is a systems-level programming construct that is not relevant in this situation or to an A+ technician.

For more information on this topic, see *A+ Exam Cram, 2nd Edition*, Chapter 11, the section "Booting and System Files".

Question 7

The correct answer is b. This is a tricky question. Some SCSI interfaces can support 15 devices, however SCSI only supports 8. The range of these addresses is 0–7. The highest number in a SCSI chain is the highest priority. Answer a is incorrect because address 8 would be an invalid address. Answer c is incorrect because address 0 is the lowest priority on the SCSI chain. Answer d is incorrect on a SCSI controller because 15 is out of the valid range of the SCSI chain. Had the question asked about a Wide SCSI adapter, answer d would be correct. Wide SCSI supports 16 devices including the controller.

For more information on this topic, see *A+ Exam Cram, 2nd Edition*, Chapter 8, the section "SCSI Interface".

Question 8

The correct answer is b. Most new motherboards provide an Accelerated Graphics Port (AGP) adapter for the video monitor adapter. Whenever possible, you should use the AGP slot. AGP provides for advanced capabilities in video technology. Answer b is incorrect; your second choice would be the Peripheral Computer Interconnect (PCI) slot. PCI provides reasonably good performance because of the high-speed capabilities of the bus. Answer c is incorrect because the Integrated Data Exchange (IDE) is designed for use by disk drives and disk type devices. Answer d is incorrect because the Integrated Systems Adaptor (ISA) is an old bus and should be used only for legacy cards that do not require extensive processor performance. The ISA bus is the oldest of the standard busses and shouldn't be used at all if you can avoid it.

For more information on this topic, see *A+ Exam Cram, 2nd Edition*, Chapter 9, the section "Basic I/O Interfaces".

Question 9

The correct answer is c. If a computer system is not retaining the system date between boots, the battery on the motherboard is almost always the culprit. Answer a is not correct; the BIOS being out of date should not be a concern. The CMOS is where BIOS data is stored and is powered by the battery. Answer b, the plug-and-play mapper, is incorrect. The mapper is called ECSD and is also powered by the battery when the system is turned off. Answer d is incorrect; refreshing the operating system will not fix this problem.

For more information on this topic, see *A+ Exam Cram, 2nd Edition*, Chapter 2, the section "System Boards: A Brief History".

Question 10

The correct answer is b. If the POST memory test fails after being left on for a while, you most likely have a bad memory unit. Answer a is incorrect and irrelevant; BIOS refresh is not something that would be affected by temperature. Answer c is incorrect; if the CPU had a heat problem, you would see a more general failure, such as the system locking up repeatedly. You can assume that if the POST starts, the CPU is working properly. Answer d is incorrect; most PCs do not need to be rebooted when they are operating normally.

For more information on this topic, see *A+ Exam Cram, 2nd Edition*, Chapter 14, the section "Hardware Problems".

Question 11

The correct answer is a. The video monitor cable and adapters for analog monitors use the DB-15 connector. Answer b is incorrect; a parallel port uses a DB-25 port. Answer c is incorrect; the USB uses a special connector that is very small. Answer d is incorrect; the serial port uses a DB-9 connector.

For more information on this topic, see *A+ Exam Cram, 2nd Edition*, Chapter 9, the section "Basic I/O Interfaces".

Question 12

The correct answer is a. The PS/2 Connector is the most common keyboard connector on AT and ATX motherboards. Answer b is incorrect; a DB-9 round connector has to the best of my knowledge never been used on a PC. Answer c is incorrect; the DB-15 is used for video monitors. Answer d is incorrect; a Molex connector is a type of connector used in power supplies and other heavier duty connections.

For more information on this topic, see *A+ Exam Cram, 2nd Edition*, Chapter 9, the section "Serial (COM) Ports: 1 Bit After Another".

Question 13

The correct answer is b. The refresh rate of a monitor is the time it takes for the beam to scan from the top to the bottom of a screen and back to the start, one full cycle. Answer a is incorrect; the sync rate is not relevant to monitors. Answer c is incorrect; masking rate is not relevant to monitors either. You will see references, while dealing with monitors, to *shadow masks*. The shadow mask is a metal sheet inside a monitor that prevents the phosphorous from glowing after it has been hit by the beam. Answer d is incorrect; frequency is a unit of measure for the rates that things occur.

For more information on this topic, see *A+ Exam Cram, 2nd Edition*, Chapter 7, the section "Screen Size".

Question 14

The correct answer is a. 1F0H is the address for the primary IDE controller. You will sometimes see the address with the H at the end and sometimes not. The H at the end of an address indicates that the address is represented in hexadecimal, or base 16. The largest number in hexadecimal is F. Answer b is incorrect; 2H0F is an invalid address. Remember that the largest number that can be represented in a hexadecimal number is F; H is not a legal number representation. Answer c is incorrect for the same reason that b is incorrect. Answer d is incorrect; address 3BEF is a valid address but not a valid driver I/O address by default.

For more information on this topic, see *A+ Exam Cram, 2nd Edition*, Chapter 5, the section "IRQS, DMA, and I/O Ports".

Question 15

The correct answer is a. Most modems provide a connection to the phone line with an RJ-11 connector. RJ-11 is a standard introduced by the phone companies for telecommunications connections. Answer b is incorrect. In our environment, most of the time an RJ-45 is used for either complicated phone systems or for a data network cable. Answer c and d are incorrect because DB-15 and DB-25 connections are digital connections, as opposed to an RJ-11, which is an analog connection. The RJ in these designations stands for Registered Jack. RJ-11 and RJ-45 connections are not universally accepted and are not as common in Europe or in Asia. Many companies sell universal telecommunications kits to allow modems to connect to foreign telephone systems.

For more information on this topic, see *A+ Exam Cram, 2nd Edition*, Chapter 9, the section "Network Cables and Connectors".

Question 16

The correct answer is b. The **ATZ** command resets the modem to the initial state that was set up by the software. Answer a is incorrect; the **ATH** command hangs up your modem. Answer c is incorrect; the **ATDT** command is used to load a phone number and make a call. Answer d is incorrect; the **+++** command is used to get the attention of the modem command processor.

For more information on this topic, see *A+ Exam Cram, 2nd Edition*, Chapter 5, the section "Modems".

Question 17

The correct answer is b. You can use one of the USB ports for one device. You can then connect a hub to the other USB port, allowing you to add multiple devices to the USB subsystem. The USB standard allows for support of up to 127 devices attached to the port. Answer a is incorrect because you can connect multiple devices to a USB port using hubs. Answer c is incorrect because you can't cross jumper USB ports. Answer d is incorrect because IEEE 1394 or Firewire is not compatible with USB. Firewire is a similar type of port connection used for high-bandwidth devices such as cameras. Many high-end systems provide connections to both USB and IEEE 1394.

For more information on this topic, see *A+ Exam Cram, 2nd Edition*, Chapter 8, the section "Universal Serial Bus (USB)".

Question 18

The correct answer is c. A UPS provides protection from power surges, power sags, and temporary power blackouts. Answer a is incorrect; Electronic Data Interchange (EDI) is not a problem but a protocol for data interchange between companies. Answer b is incorrect; Electronic Static Discharge (ESD) is an atmospheric condition and is not changed by the UPS. Answer d is incorrect; Electro Magnetic Interference (EMI) is interference caused by radio frequency or other transmissions. Computer systems as well as devices such as microwave ovens, CB radios, and electrical machinery generate EMI.

For more information on this topic, see *A+ Exam Cram, 2nd Edition*, Chapter 5, the section "Basic Electronics".

Question 19

The correct answer is c. The 301 error is the code for a keyboard failure. Answer a is incorrect; memory failures are vendor specific but most BIOS processes provide a plain language indicator during the memory test. Answer b is incorrect; a power supply failure will generally prevent the system from starting correctly. Answer d is incorrect; floppy drives do not provide a default POST error, although the floppy controller does.

For more information on this topic, see *A+ Exam Cram, 2ⁿᵈ Edition*, Chapter 14, the section "Boot Problems".

Question 20

The correct answer is a. One of the nicest features of USB is the ability to hot add and remove devices. When you do this, the operating system will automatically run a hardware installation wizard for configuration. When you remove a device from a USB port, the system will automatically deactivate the driver. You do not have to reboot or shutdown a computer to change USB configuration. Configuration changes are made dynamically. Answer b is incorrect; USB does not require a reboot in the event of configuration change. Answer c is incorrect; the USB port does not have any interaction with the BIOS; it is handled through the operating system. Answer d is incorrect; USB allows for hot swapping.

For more information on this topic, see *A+ Exam Cram, 2ⁿᵈ Edition*, Chapter 8, the section "Universal Serial Bus (USB)".

Question 21

The correct answer is a. A sure symptom of a ribbon wearing out is fuzz being present on the paper. This fuzz is material being shed from the ribbon. If you replace the ribbon and still observe fuzz on the paper, you probably have a stuck printer pin. Sometimes cleaning the print head will free the print pin. If that does not work, you will need to replace the print head. Answer b is incorrect; replacing the ribbon without cleaning the print head may leave material on the print head and cause it to jam. Answer c is incorrect; changing the paper will not prevent printer ribbon deterioration. Answer d is incorrect; you do not know if the print head is defective until you clean it and change the ribbon.

For more information on this topic, see *A+ Exam Cram, 2ⁿᵈ Edition*, Chapter 7, the section "Dot Matrix".

Question 22

The correct answer is b. The Extended Capability Port (ECP) is the fastest parallel or printer port used on PCs. Answer a is incorrect; Standard Parallel Port (SPP) is one of the oldest and most common port standards, but it is not fast. Answer c is incorrect; the Enhanced Parallel Port (EPP) is very fast but not as fast as the ECP but still faster than the SPP. The parallel ports are bidirectional, which means that they can be used to send or receive data. Many lower-end scanners and devices such as Zip drives can use the parallel port for connection to the PC. Answer d is incorrect; Bisynchronous Data Interconnect (BSDI) is not a parallel port mode.

For more information on this topic, see *A+ Exam Cram, 2nd Edition*, Chapter 9, the section "Parallel (LPT) Ports: 8 Bits Across".

Question 23

The correct answer is c. The 100BaseT network has a transfer rate of 100 megabits per second (Mbps) across a cable. Cat 5 is the only choice given for a cable that has the certification for 100Mbps. Answer a is incorrect; Cat 1 is useful for very low speed networks and generally not used for data cabling. Answer c is incorrect; CAT 3 cabling is useful for maximum transfer rate 10Mbps data transfer rate. Answer d is incorrect; CAT 10 cable is not a meaningful standard for cable at this point.

For more information on this topic, see *A+ Exam Cram, 2nd Edition*, Chapter 9, the section "Network Cables and Connectors".

Question 24

The correct answer is b. A 10BaseT has a maximum cable length of 100 meters. Answer a is incorrect; 50 meters is within the length of a 10BaseT network. Answers c and d are incorrect; 10BaseT networks do not have a length of 200 meters or 385 meters. Twisted pair cable is susceptible to interference and the longer the length, the more interference and attenuation and signal distortion become a factor. Some cables, if of high quality, may work for longer lengths, but in general, for reliability purposes, you shouldn't "push the envelope" on this. Interference and attenuation problems can be very difficult and tricky to troubleshoot. If you need to exceed the 100-meter length, you can always add a hub to the line. Hubs recondition the line and you could effectively double the distance of the cable by doing this.

For more information on this topic, see *A+ Exam Cram, 2nd Edition*, Chapter 9, the section "Network Cables and Connectors".

Question 25

The correct answer is a. A 10Base2 network uses a coaxial cable and is bus oriented. Answer b is incorrect; a star network uses a central hub and spoke configuration. Answer c is incorrect; a ring network sends the data via a token in a round robin manner through the network. Answer d is incorrect; a mesh is a type of network that has multiple paths between systems. Mesh networks can be implemented using multiple network cards in some or all of the computer systems. These network adapters can be connected to create a fish net effect so that multiple paths exist between the systems on the network.

For more information on this topic, see *A+ Exam Cram, 2nd Edition*, Chapter 8, the section "Networking Overview".

Question 26

The correct answer is b. A 10BaseT network is a star-oriented network. Each of the network adapters is connected through cable to a hub. Hubs can be connected to each other through other hubs, which allows for easy fault isolation and keeps the systems isolated. Most networks being installed in businesses today use a star-based topology or method. Answer a is incorrect; a bus network connects all of the network devices to a single cable (usually coax). Bus networks are simple to implement in smaller networks, and network stations are connected using co-axial T adapters to the cable. Answer c is incorrect; a ring network passes data from one machine to the next in a closed loop or ring. Ring networks could be bidirectional, allowing some data path redundancy. Answer d is incorrect; mesh networks are hybrids that use one or more of the methods described here.

For more information on this topic, see *A+ Exam Cram, 2nd Edition*, Chapter 8, the section "Networking Overview".

Question 27

The correct answer is b. Fast/Wide SCSI supports 15 devices and the controller. Be careful how you read this type of question. A SCSI bus always supports at least 7 devices and a controller. Fast/Wide SCSI supports 16 devices, in contrast to SCSI, which only supports 8. The *fast* designation merely defines the performance characteristic of the bus. Answer a is incorrect; Fast SCSI supports 8 devices including the controller. Answer c is incorrect; the controller always uses one connection. Answer d is incorrect; at this time Wide SCSI only supports 16 devices.

For more information on this topic, see *A+ Exam Cram, 2nd Edition*, Chapter 6, the section "Hard Drive Configuration".

Question 28

The correct answer is a. L1 cache is contained in the CPU. Answer b is incorrect; L II cache is on the motherboard. Answers c and d are incorrect; Level III and hash cache are not meaningful in this example.

For more information on this topic, see *A+ Exam Cram, 2nd Edition*, Chapter 3, the section "L-1 and L-2 Caches".

Question 29

The correct answer is b. IRQ 3 is the default for COM2. Answer a is incorrect; IRQ 2 is used to connect or cascade to IRQ 9. Answer c is incorrect; COM1 uses IRQ 4. Answer d is incorrect; the keyboard uses IRQ 1.

For more information on this topic, see *A+ Exam Cram, 2nd Edition*, Chapter 5, the section "IRQs, DMA, and I/O Ports".

Question 30

The correct answer is c. A half-duplex connection allows for two-way communications but in only one direction at a time. The closest example of this is a two-way radio. When one person is talking to the other, he or she depresses the microphone transmit switch and starts talking. This turns off the receiver on the transmitter side. When the transmitter is done, he or she says "over" and releases the key, which allows the other side to transmit. Answer a is incorrect; full-duplex communications can occur in both directions simultaneously. Your telephone is an example of full-duplex communications. Answer b is incorrect, asynchronous communications means that both sides of the connection can communicate simultaneously. Answer d is incorrect; a bisynchronous communication has no meaningful definition in this situation.

For more information on this topic, see *A+ Exam Cram, 2nd Edition*, Chapter 9, the section "Serial (COM) Ports: 1 Bit after Another".

Question 31

The correct answer is b. When you install a new hard drive, you must first logically define how the drive is used. In Windows, you use the FDISK program to partition the physical disk into one or more logical partitions. These partitions can then be formatted using the appropriate program for storage. Answer a is incorrect; if the hard disk is not recognized by FDISK, it is likely that it has been configured incorrectly or is defective. Answer c is incorrect; CHKDSK is a utility that allows for the media to be scanned and errors corrected. One of the areas on a bootable drive is the Master Boot Record (MBR). Answer d is incorrect; SCANDISK is another drive utility that can be used to verify the health of a disk drive. A surface analysis is an extensive and exhaustive diagnostic process where each physical location on the disk is checked to verify that it is working properly. The surface analysis on a large disk can take many hours. If you are having sporadic disk problems or suspect that your disk drive is acting up, you should do a surface analysis of the drive to verify its health.

For more information on this topic, see *A+ Exam Cram, 2nd Edition*, Chapter 6, the section "Fixed Disks/Hard Drives".

Question 32

The correct answer is d. The boot priority of the drives is probably set incorrectly and needs to be changed. A normal boot order is *a: c: CD-ROM*. Answer a is incorrect; the **Format** program on the hard drive would erase all of the data on the disk and prepare it for storage. You should run **Format** cautiously and double-check all of your answers. Once you start a **Format**, it is usually unstoppable. A very common customer-service issue is a customer inadvertently formatting a hard drive. As a general rule, this process is irreversible. Answer b is incorrect; formatting the floppy disk would not address the hard drive boot up issue. Answer c is incorrect; you can only change the BIOS settings during startup of the computer. You cannot generally alter the boot sequence anywhere but during BIOS setup.

For more information on this topic, see *A+ Exam Cram, 2nd Edition*, Chapter 11, the section "Booting and System Files".

Question 33

The correct answer is b. You can usually install additional IDE controllers into expansion slots to add more drives. It is highly recommended that you use PCI expansion if available; it will provide the highest performance. Answer a is incorrect; adding an additional controller would allow adding drives. Answer c is incorrect; no such animal exists to create a three-connection IDE cable—it wouldn't work anyway as the maximum addressing capability of an IDE controller is two devices. Answer d is incorrect; you cannot interconnect floppy and hard drives.

For more information on this topic, see *A+ Exam Cram, 2nd Edition*, Chapter 6, the section "Hard Drive Controllers".

Question 34

The correct answer is c. A very common problem is that the floppy drive may have a higher precedence in the boot sequence than the hard drive. If a floppy that is not bootable is in drive a:, the system may hang or give an error message. Most systems will issue an error message in this case, but some do not. Verify that all media except the bootable media has been removed from the system. Answer a is incorrect; if the system were not plugged in, you would not get a successful POST indication. Answer b is incorrect; the hard drive may have failed but this is not as likely as nonbootable media interfering with the boot up process. Answer d is incorrect; unmounting a device is not a function available to Windows operating systems for CD-ROMs. You can eject a CD-ROM, which may also be interfering with the boot process.

For more information on this topic, see *A+ Exam Cram, 2nd Edition*, Chapter 11, the section "Booting and System Files".

Question 35

The correct answers are a, b, and c. Basic troubleshooting techniques dictate that you should verify the power source and all related areas. The customer will, in most cases, swear that cables and connections are correct. If the customer has verified the power connections, you should also have them verify that the wall receptacle is working. You would want to verify all switches are turned on; all power connections are plugged in and operational. Surge suppressers can often cause time to be wasted in troubleshooting systems problems. You should verify that the surge suppresser is working and the breaker on the suppresser has not popped. (Customer service personnel have received support calls from customers during black outs wondering why the computer system is malfunctioning.) You would only replace a power supply after you have verified that everything else is working and plugged in correctly. Answer d is a possibility but not as likely as one of the other choices. A good question sequence to ask: "Is it plugged in? Is it plugged in on the other end?" You may be surprised how often this will fix the problem and avoid a service call.

For more information on this topic, see *A+ Exam Cram, 2nd Edition*, Chapter 14, the section "Hardware Problems".

Question 36

The correct answers are a, b, and c. The Pentium II, Pentium III and Celeron chips use the slot 1 socket. Answer d is incorrect; the PIII Xeon uses a slot 2 socket.

For more information on this topic, see *A+ Exam Cram, 2nd Edition*, Chapter 3, the section "Pentium Processors".

Question 37

The correct answer is a. A battery backup is also known as a Uninterruptible Power Supply (UPS). Answer b is incorrect; surge suppressers are designed to prevent damage from line surges or sags. Answer c is incorrect; a voltage regulator keeps the voltage on a line constant as long as the voltage is present. Voltage regulators are useful if you have unstable line voltage. Some UPS systems also can provide voltage regulation. Answer d is incorrect; an ESD eliminator might also be called a ground wire. ESD is a condition where high voltage static electricity discharges across a circuit, potentially causing component damage.

For more information on this topic, see *A+ Exam Cram, 2nd Edition*, Chapter 3, the section "Central Processing Unit (CPU)".

Question 38

The correct answer is a. The ISA bus has an 8- or 16-bit data width. Answer b is incorrect; EISA has a 32-bit capability but can also accept older ISA cards. Answer c is incorrect; an 8-16-32-bit bus is the standard bus size for a Micro Channel Architecture (MCA). PCI also operates on a 32-bit bus. Answer d is incorrect; PCI-2, a fairly new bus, has a 64-bit data width.

For more information on this topic, see *A+ Exam Cram, 2nd Edition*, Chapter 2, the section "Industry Standard Architecture (ISA)".

Question 39

The correct answer is a. A DIMM memory card has 64-bit data width and only requires 1 card per row. Answer b is incorrect; SIMM memory is 32-bit and would require 2 cards per bank. Answers c and d are not valid in Pentium processors. Most modern motherboards use the DIMM socket for computer memory, although some older boards provided the ability to use either SIMM or DIMM memory.

For more information on this topic, see *A+ Exam Cram, 2nd Edition*, Chapter 4, the section "Packaging Modules".

Question 40

The correct answer is b. During the process of normal use on a hard drive, files are added and deleted. Over time, this will cause gaps or holes in the storage space on the hard drive. As this gets worse, system performance can be severely impacted. I recommend that you run a defragramentation program on a system on a regular basis: weekly or monthly. Answer a is incorrect; running FDISK would cause the disk to lose its partition information and effectively erase the hard disk partition. Answer c is incorrect; disk compression is a mechanism where the files are squished and space is freed up. Disk compression allows for more data to be stored on a disk than would normally be capable at the cost of system performance. It takes processor time to compress and uncompress disk files, thus causing slower performance. Answer d is incorrect; if you ran **Format** on a FAT disk, you would erase the data stored on a logical drive. This would blank out the disk and would require a restore to be done to get the data back. This will effectively defrag a disk but is very time-consuming process and offers a higher opportunity to lose data.

For more information on this topic, see *A+ Exam Cram, 2nd Edition,* Chapter 10, the section "DEFRAG.EXE".

Question 41

The correct answer is c. When you move or install a system, make sure that all the cables are screwed back in. Video monitor cables being loose can cause the monitor to blank out or change colors when touched. While answer a is possible, it is not the most likely scenario. If the cables are tight and the problem persists, you should then check the video card to verify that it hasn't come loose inside the system. Answer b is incorrect; a defective monitor might cause this type of problem, but because you just moved the system, a loose cable is more likely. Answer d is also incorrect. Power sags might cause a monitor to display unusual characteristics but you would notice lights dimming and other unusual environmental issues.

For more information on this topic, see *A+ Exam Cram, 2nd Edition,* Chapter 7, the section "Video Displays".

Question 42

The correct answer is c. The address of LPT2 is 0278. Answer a is incorrect; the address of COM1 is 03E8. Answer b is incorrect; the address of COM4 is 02E8. Answer d is incorrect; the address of LPT1 is 0378. You should commit the Input/Output (I/O) addresses of the COM and LPT ports to memory; you will most likely encounter one or more of these on the A+ exam.

For more information on this topic, see *A+ Exam Cram, 2nd Edition,* Chapter 5, the section "IRQs, DMA, and I/O Ports".

Question 43

The correct answers are a, b, and c. To get the longest life from a UPS or battery backup put only the items essential for operation on the UPS. In the case of a server, you can leave the monitor off, as it is not needed for normal operation. Answer c is incorrect because keyboards receive power from the system unit and do not require separate power.

For more information on this topic, see *A+ Exam Cram, 2nd Edition,* Chapter 9, the section "Serial (COM) Ports: 1 Bit after Another".

Question 44

The correct answer is c. A class C fire extinguisher is suitable for fire suppression on electrical systems such as PCs, surge suppressors, and UPS systems. Answer a is incorrect; class A fire extinguishers are usually water based and designed for wood or paper products. Answer b is incorrect; class B extinguishers are suitable for grease or fueled fires such as gasoline or grease. Answer d is incorrect; class D extinguishers are intended for metallic fires and are usually rated for specific metals. Using the wrong rating of fire extinguisher may be ineffective and potentially hazardous to the operator of the extinguisher. For example, a class A fire extinguisher might not put out an electrical fire and might also raise shock potential to the user.

For more information on this topic, see the Hanford Fire Department Web site at **www.hanford.gov/fire/safety/extingrs.htm**.

Question 45

The correct answers are a and b. ISA and EISA bus standards have been largely replaced by PCI bus on computer systems. Many devices that used ISA in the past are not available as USB devices or PCI. Answer c and d are incorrect; whenever possible you should use PCI or USB over ISA. ISA and EISA bus standards place a much higher demand on the microprocessor than the other busses in use today.

For more information on this topic, see *A+ Exam Cram, 2nd Edition,* Chapter 2, the section "Expansion Bus Architecture".

Question 46

The correct answer is c. The modern AT or Pentium system provides 8 Direct Memory Access (DMA) channels for devices. DMA allows the machine to move data from one place to another without involving the CPU, thus improving system performance. Answer a is incorrect; no PC ever had only 2 DMA channels. Answer b is incorrect; early PC systems had 4 DMA channels. Answer d is incorrect; DMA is alive and well and will stay in PCs for years to come.

For more information on this topic, see *A+ Exam Cram, 2nd Edition*, Chapter 5, the section "Direct Memory Access (DMA) Channels".

Question 47

The correct answer is a. A Type 3 PC Card has a width of 10.5 mm. Virtually all portable PC systems allow for only one Type 3 card in the PC Card slot. A Type 1 card has a width of 3.5 mm. A Type 2 card has a width of 5 mm. As you can deduce from this, most systems will allow for any combination of two Type 1 or Type 2 cards and that the width of the PC card slots in a portable would be at least 10.5 mm. Answers b, c, and d are incorrect because the overall width of these combinations of cards would exceed 10.5 mm.

For more information on this topic, see *A+ Exam Cram, 2nd Edition*, Chapter 2, the section "PC Card (PCMCIA)".

Question 48

The correct answer is a. The USB port uses only one IRQ. This allows for the connection of a large number of devices to the USB port without tying up precious IRQs. Answers b, c and d are incorrect because the USB only uses one IRQ address.

For more information on this topic, see *A+ Exam Cram, 2nd Edition*, Chapter 8, the section "Universal Serial Bus (USB)".

Question 49

The correct answers are a, b, and c. USB allows for easy configuration, high speed data processing, and hot swapping. Answer d is incorrect; USB does not allow for any fault tolerance of devices on the USB.

For more information on this topic, see *A+ Exam Cram, 2nd Edition*, Chapter 8, the section "Universal Serial Bus (USB)".

Question 50

The correct answers are a, b, and d. One of the nicest features of USB is the variety of devices becoming available for it. You can find multimedia devices, monitors, printers, and mice available for USB. Answer c is incorrect; at this point I am not aware of a SCSI disk that will connect into a USB port, although you can buy SCSI adapters to plug into the USB port. With USB, upgrades to a system can be done in many cases without opening the case.

For more information on this topic, see *A+ Exam Cram, 2nd Edition,* Chapter 8, the section "Universal Serial Bus (USB)".

Question 51

The correct answers are c and d. Scanners and hard drives are two of the primary types of devices for connection to the SCSI bus. You will also find CD-ROMs, DVDs, and tape backup systems available on SCSI. Answers a and b are incorrect; a SCSI modem would be a horribly inefficient use of a SCSI bus. Printers generally either use a USB, LPT, or COM connection. Many new scanners provide both SCSI and USB connections for maximum configuration flexibility. In the future, it is highly probable that most scanner manufacturers will discontinue the SCSI interface entirely and stick with the USB port as the primary connection.

For more information on this topic, see *A+ Exam Cram, 2nd Edition,* Chapter 8, the section "SCSI Interface".

Question 52

The correct answer is c. A USB port can support up to 127 devices. It would probably become a plumber's nightmare if you tried to hook up this many devices, but theoretically it is 127. Answers a, b, and d are incorrect because 127 is the correct answer.

For more information on this topic, see *A+ Exam Cram, 2nd Edition,* Chapter 8, the section "Universal Serial Bus (USB)".

Question 53

The correct answer is a. Most PDAs allow for message transmission between each other and printers using an infrared port (IR). You generally select the document you want to send, aim the PDA at the receiver, and press the Send button. IR is suitable mostly for small files and documents because the bandwidth is fairly low. Answer b is incorrect, but certainly a possibility. Many PDAs now include a USB connection, which allows you to connect the PDA to a PC or other device. For sending small documents, you would generally use the IR port. Answer c is incorrect because you can purchase LAN cards for PDA devices to enable them to connect to a wire or wireless network. Answer d is incorrect; FTP is a file transfer protocol used extensively on the Internet.

For more information on this topic, see *A+ Exam Cram, 2ⁿᵈ Edition,* Chapter 9, the section "Network Cables and Connectors".

Question 54

The correct answer is d. Most motherboards that support both SIMM and DIMM memory do not allow them to be interchanged. You usually have to either select DIMM or SIMM. This was provided as a way to allow for inexpensive upgrades using existing SIMM memory. At the time of this writing, DIMM memory is very inexpensive and is the prevalent type of memory used in PC systems today. Answer a is incorrect; a bad memory module is a possibility but not as likely as mixed memory. Normally, POST would catch a memory problem on the motherboard. Answer b is incorrect; a bad power supply would provide you with a different type of error and would not affect one type of memory more than another. Answer c is incorrect; a memory conflict in the bank switches is not a good choice either. Older motherboards had memory bank switching to indicate which slots had memory in them and which didn't. One of the nicest features of DIMM memory, in particular, is the elimination of bank switches on motherboards.

For more information on this topic, see *A+ Exam Cram, 2ⁿᵈ Edition,* Chapter 4, the section "Packaging Modules".

Question 55

The correct answer is c. The bus width of a PCI card is 32 bits. This, in conjunction with its high bus speed, is why PCI is preferable over the ISA or EISA busses. Answer a is incorrect; the original ISA cards had a bus width of 8 bits. Answer b is incorrect; later ISA cards had a 16-bit bus. Answer d is incorrect. Although a 64-bit bus is available under a new standard called PCI-2, PCI-2 is not yet common on PC systems.

For more information on this topic, see *A+ Exam Cram, 2ⁿᵈ Edition,* Chapter 2, the section "Peripheral Component Interconnect (PCI)".

Question 56

The correct answers are a and d. Synchronous Dynamic Random Access Memory (SDRAM) offers burst data transfers and dynamic refresh. Burst data transfers means that small amounts of data can be sent to the bus at very fast speeds. Dynamic refresh refers to the fact that the memory contents must be recycled internally every few instruction cycles or the contents will be lost. Answer b is incorrect; dynamic RAM is slower than static RAM but costs considerably less and uses less power. Answer c is incorrect; all RAM is volatile in that it does not retain its content when power is removed.

For more information on this topic, see *A+ Exam Cram, 2nd Edition*, Chapter 4, the section "A RAM Game".

Question 57

The correct answer is b. If a terminator in a bus network such as 10Base2 becomes defective or is removed, the network will become unstable and will probably stop functioning. This problem would remove access to shares, printers, and other network resources. Answer a is incorrect; bus networks do not use hubs. Answer c is incorrect; most networks do not have power supplies on the cable as the signal—the network adapters and terminators provide conditioning. Answer d is incorrect; a server malfunctioning and going offline would certainly cause resources to become unavailable; however, in this scenario, you are working with multiple servers. A single failure of a server would not cause the entire network to become inoperable except in very rare cases.

For more information on this topic, see *A+ Exam Cram, 2nd Edition*, Chapter 9, the section "Network Cables and Connectors".

Question 58

The correct answer is b. The fusing stage of a laser printer is where the ink or toner is melted onto the paper. Answer a is incorrect; the charging phase prepares the paper to accept the toner by charging the paper with a high voltage. Answer c is incorrect; the discharging stage is where the drum and charge on the paper are discharged in preparation for the fusing stage. Answer d is incorrect; the transfer phase is where the toner or ink is transferred from the drum to the paper and a visible image is seen on the paper.

For more information on this topic, see *A+ Exam Cram, 2nd Edition*, Chapter 7, the section "Laser Printers".

Question 59

The correct answer is a. Normally, a 10BaseT network uses a hub to connect systems together. If you had a network where only two computers were connected, you could use a crossover cable to connect them together and eliminate the hub. This would work in a situation only where you had two computers to connect. Answer b is incorrect; a CAT 5 normal cable is used to connect computers and hubs together in the normal manner. Answer c is incorrect; an RS232 null modem cable is a type of cable used to connect serial ports together. Answer d is incorrect; an IEEE 4888 cable is a special type of network connection and has no bearing on the CAT 5 cabling.

For more information on this topic, see *A+ Exam Cram, 2nd Edition,* Chapter 9, the section "Network Cables and Connectors".

Question 60

The correct answer is c. If you are seeing only half a printed character on a page, you should assume that the platen or printing surface has become misaligned. Usually you can realign this fairly simply (consult the owner's manual to determine the steps to do this). Answer a is incorrect; when a print head malfunctions, it is not unusual for the entire head to just stop printing, rendering no meaningful output. Answer b is incorrect; a paper misalignment may cause a printing problem but is usually quite evident when you inspect the printer. Answer d is incorrect; a paper limiting switch malfunction might cause your printer to constantly think it is out of paper or has a paper jam, preventing the paper from advancing.

For more information on this topic, see *A+ Exam Cram, 2nd Edition,* Chapter 7, the section "Printer Problems".

Question 61

The correct answer is c. A workgroup is a type of network that involves each workstation being potentially both a server of resources and a user of other workstation resources. A simple way to keep this straight is to remember that if a network has dedicated servers, it is not a peer-to-peer network. Answer a is incorrect; some networks have a server whose entire function is to manage the network resources, including accounts, naming conventions, resources, etc. The server that does this is called a domain server and establishes a clear security boundary between the network and outsiders. Answer b is incorrect; a client-server network is a type of network that has servers dedicated to providing access to data and other resources using servers to provide the data. A client-server environment allows for workstations to be unconcerned about where the physical resources are located, because the workstation merely talks to the server for information. Answer d is incorrect; 10BaseT is a type of network topology that uses twisted-pair connections and is star oriented.

For more information on this topic, see *A+ Exam Cram, 2nd Edition*, Chapter 8, the section "Networking Overview".

Question 62

The correct answer is b. Intel introduced MultiMedia Extensions (MMX) to Pentium processors to speed up multimedia on computer systems. The MMX instruction set is optimized for efficient access to these types of instructions. Answers a and c are incorrect; MMX only improves multimedia processing. MMX processors do not perform other operations such as math or comparisons any faster than non-MMX based processors. Answer d is incorrect; floating-point operations refer to the operations involving noninteger mathematics. Floating-point arithmetic is not faster using MMX technology.

For more information on this topic, see *A+ Exam Cram, 2nd Edition*, Chapter 3, the section "Pentium Processors".

Question 63

The correct answer is c. Most dot-matrix printers use a set of guides to pull the paper through the print area across the printing surface. Tractor feeds are attached to the paper and keep the paper flowing across the platen smoothly. Answer a is incorrect; pressure feed is not normally used on dot-matrix printers. Pressure feed involves a tension between the platen and a roller to pull paper into the printer. Answer b is incorrect; vacuum feed has been used in very fast printers but is not something you will typically encounter in a normal office environment or on a dot-matrix printer. Answer d is incorrect; gravity feed is not used on dot-matrix printers and seldom used on printers at all.

For more information on this topic, see *A+ Exam Cram, 2nd Edition*, Chapter 7, the section "Dot Matrix".

Question 64

The correct answer is d. The control unit manages all the functions of the printing process in a laser printer. Answer a is incorrect; the fusing unit melts the toner onto the paper at the end of the printing process. If the fusing unit had malfunctioned, the toner would not be melted onto the paper and you would have an image on the page but it would not be permanent. Answer b is incorrect, if the static discharge had malfunctioned, the paper would not have had any printable characters on it, as the roller would have retained the ink and none would have been transferred to the paper. Answer c is incorrect; the scavenger bar is intended to scrape any unneeded toner off the printer drum and returns it to the toner cartridge.

For more information on this topic, see *A+ Exam Cram, 2nd Edition*, Chapter 7, the section "Laser Printers".

Question 65

The correct answer is a. Windows RAM (WRAM) is used for video memory. Answer b is incorrect; cache memory is usually found either in the processor or on the motherboard near the processor. Answer c is incorrect; DIMM memory is also typically found on the motherboard in proximity to the processor. Answer d is incorrect; PCI bus accelerator memory is something that sounded good for this question. WRAM is most typically located on the video or AGP card.

For more information on this topic, see *A+ Exam Cram, 2nd Edition*, Chapter 4, the section "Types of RAM".

Question 66

The correct answers are a and c. The most typical measure of speed in a dot-matrix printer is characters per second (CPS). It is not unusual for a dot-matrix to be able to print 8 or 10 characters per second. (Faster dot matrix printers sound like a box of mad cats all screaming at once as the print head is dragged across the paper and the pins are projected from the print head.) The other common measure of performance in dot-matrix printers is lines per minute (LPM), which refers to the number of lines that the printer can print per minute. Answer b is incorrect; Pages per minute (PPM) is a measure of band printers and refers to the number of pages per minute that can be printed. Answer d is incorrect; CPM or Characters per minute in not a measurement used for printer speeds.

For more information on this topic, see *A+ Exam Cram, 2nd Edition*, Chapter 7, the section "Dot Matrix".

Question 67

The correct answer is b. In 10BaseT, as well as 100BaseT, the 10 or 100 refer to how many megabits (or millions of bits) per second (Mbps) of data is transferred across the network. Answer a is incorrect; cable length limits on these types of networks are 100 meters and established by the network standard. Answer c is incorrect; megabytes (MB) refer to millions of bytes, which are 8 bits of data at a time. Answer d is incorrect; IRQ/DMA pairing has nothing to do with the 10/100 designations on a NIC card.

For more information on this topic, see *A+ Exam Cram, 2nd Edition*, Chapter 8, the section "Networking Overview".

Question 68

The correct answers are a and b. 10BaseT and 100BaseT use a network connector that is similar to a telephone connector. The connector is identified as an RJ-45 connection. Telephones most typically use an RJ-11 connection. RJ stands for *registered jack* and is a common designator for telephone and data transmission. Answer c is incorrect; 10Base2 is a coaxial network that uses a British Naval Connector (BNC) for connections to a device. Answer d is incorrect; 1Base10 is a fictitious network protocol, as far as I know.

For more information on this topic, see *A+ Exam Cram, 2nd Edition*, Chapter 8, the section "Networking Overview".

Question 69

The correct answer is a. The primary measurement normally used in evaluating the capacity of a power supply is watts. A watt is a unit of energy. A typical power supply in a PC can handle about 250 watts. Answer b is incorrect; voltage is one of the factors in calculating wattage but refers to the line voltage of the power supply, either on the input or output side. Answer c is incorrect; amperage (Amps) is the measure of current that a line can provide or carry. Power is calculated by the following formula: Power = Voltage × Current. Answer d is incorrect; resistance is an electronic term relative to the value of a device's ability to consume power. Resistance is measured in ohms.

For more information on this topic, see *A+ Exam Cram, 2nd Edition*, Chapter 5, the section "Basic Electronics".

Question 70

The correct answer is a. 03E8H is the normal address for I/O for COM3. Answer b is incorrect; the normal address for COM4 is 02F8H. Answers c and d are incorrect; they do not refer to COM addresses.

For more information on this topic, see *A+ Exam Cram, 2nd Edition*, Chapter 5, the section "IRQs, DMA, and I/O Ports".

A+ OS Technologies Practice Test #1

Question 1

Of the following, which shares will not show up on the network by default?

○ a. 'Hidden1'

○ b. 'Ghost1'

○ c. 'InvisibleMan'

○ d. 'C$'

Question 2

You are experiencing very long waits for Web pages at the office. What tool can you use to check for time lags between you and the Web pages you are viewing?

○ a. COMMAND.COM

○ b. AppleTalk

○ c. Remote Access Service

○ d. Tracert

Question 3

When you save a document while working on Windows 2000, where is it saved by default?

- ○ a. C:\System32\Temp
- ○ b. C:\DeskTop\Temp
- ○ c. C:\Documents and settings
- ○ d. C:\Program Files\Documents and files

Question 4

You are copying files from one drive to the other when the message "This directory contains 3 hidden files" appears. What will happen to the hidden files if you choose Select All again and then perform the paste?

- ○ a. All files will be copied.
- ○ b. Only the files that are not hidden will be copied.
- ○ c. The view will include the hidden files.
- ○ d. The hidden files will be copied into a separate directory.

Question 5

Which term best describes the way to organize common files?

- ○ a. Format
- ○ b. Folder
- ○ c. FDISK
- ○ d. F5

Question 6

If the directory table has run out of room on the root directory, which of the following errors are you likely to receive?

○ a. "Invalid Command"

○ b. "Insufficient Disk Space"

○ c. "General Protection Fault in Kernl386.exe"

○ d. "Duplicate File name Exists"

Question 7

If you are six levels deep into a directory tree, which command can you enter at the DOS prompt to return you to the root directory?

○ a. **CD .**

○ b. **CD ..**

○ c. **Root**

○ d. **CD **

Question 8

Along with the File Allocation Table, what other tracking is used for directories?

○ a. V-FAT

○ b. V-DAT

○ c. DAT

○ d. FAT-32

Question 9

Which of the following best describes the function of DEFRAG.EXE?

○ a. Keeps files in contiguous areas.

○ b. Keeps files in separate directories.

○ c. Must be run only in Windows.

○ d. Stores Long File Names.

Question 10

Which of the following commands issued from the DOS prompt are most likely to return a "File Not Found" response?

○ a. **Dir/s mydoc.doc**

○ b. **Dir/a mydoc.txt**

○ c. **Dir mydoc.rtf**

○ d. **Dir/s mydoc**

Question 11

Windows 2000 supports how many USB devices?

○ a. 7

○ b. 27

○ c. 127

○ d. 227

Question 12

A network composed entirely of Windows 98 systems would be considered which type of network?

○ a. Client/server

○ b. Star topology

○ c. Bus topology

○ d. Peer-to-peer

Question 13

Which of the following standards identifies an Ethernet Network?

○ a. IEEE 802.3

○ b. IEEE 802.5

○ c. IEEE 805.2

○ d. IEEE 803.2

Question 14

What is the maximum number of workstations Microsoft recommends for a bus network?

○ a. 10

○ b. 20

○ c. 50

○ d. 100

Question 15

When computers on a network are placed together in such a way that they are all connected to a single cable, what is the topology of that type of network?

○ a. Ring

○ b. Bus

○ c. Star

○ d. Mesh

Question 16

Which layer of the OSI model is actually two layers combined?

○ a. Physical

○ b. Data Link

○ c. Network

○ d. Transport

Question 17

Of the following, ISDN connections support how much bandwidth over an ordinary phone line?

○ a. 1.5Mbps

○ b. 256Kbps

○ c. 128Mbps

○ d. 128Kbps

Question 18

The **ATTRIB** command in DOS does which of the following?

○ a. Sets or removes attributes.

○ b. Prevents attributes from being changed on the target file.

○ c. Sets the modem to respond with a "Ring in Busy" signal.

○ d. Provides the **BACKUP** command with a list of file attributes.

Question 19

Which of the statements in the AUTOEXEC.BAT will not provide a valid path to C:\Windows?

○ a. **Path=C:\; C:\DOS; C:\Windows**

○ b. **Path= C:\Windows; C:\DOS; C:**

○ c. **Path=C:**

    Path=C:\Dos; %path%

    Path=C:\Windows; %path%

○ d. **Path=C:\: C:\DOS: C:\Windows**

Question 20

When you write DOS batch files, you use the **REM** statement to remark out the line following the statement. Which of the following provides the equivalent effect in Windows INI files?

○ a. **WINREM**

○ b. **INIREM**

○ c. **%**

○ d. **;**

Question 21

In which of the following files would you most likely see the command
; DELETE=C:\\?

○ a. AUTOEXEC.BAT

○ b. CONFIG.SYS

○ c. WIN.INI

○ d. PROGMAN.EXE

Question 22

Of the following, which cannot be formatted with NTFS?

○ a. Hard drive

○ b. Floppy drive

○ c. Stripe set

○ d. Volume set

Question 23

Of the following, which cannot be converted to FAT-32 in Windows 98 using
the Drive Converter?

○ a. FAT-16

○ b. V-FAT

○ c. NTFS

○ d. Blank partition

Question 24

A customer brings his 486sx computer into your shop and complains that his games run slowly. You interview the customer and discover that he plays only DOS-based games. When you attempt to boot the computer, you receive the error message: "No operating system". What is the best way to fix this problem?

○ a. Reformat the hard drive.

○ b. Reinstall DOS.

○ c. Repartition the hard drive.

○ d. Run the **SYS** command from a bootable floppy.

Question 25

When a device has been disabled on a Windows 2000 operating system, what is the symbol shown in the Device Manager?

○ a. A yellow circle with a black exclamation point

○ b. A red x

○ c. A yellow circle with a red exclamation point

○ d. A black x

Question 26

Of the following utilities, which will improve hard disk access speed on a Windows 2000 computer?

○ a. REGEDIT.EXE

○ b. MEMMAKER.EXE

○ c. DEFRAG.EXE

○ d. CHKDSK.EXE

Question 27

When you start your Windows NT 4 Workstation, you receive the error message: "One or more services failed to start". Where should you look to determine which service(s) failed?

○ a. CMOS

○ b. Event Viewer

○ c. Task Manager

○ d. CONFIG.SYS

Question 28

You are running backups on a Windows 2000 Server of only the files that have changed since your last backup. Which type of backup are you running?

○ a. Differential

○ b. Incremental

○ c. Full

○ d. Mixed mode

Question 29

A customer calls your help line complaining that the icons on his desktop are too small. You ask the customer to right-click on the desktop, select Properties and click on the Settings tab. The customer responds that the tabs are too small to read. What is the easiest thing that should be done to ensure the desktop is being displayed at 640x480 screen resolution?

○ a. Reinstall the video adapter driver.

○ b. Reinstall the operating system.

○ c. Reboot the operating system in Safe Mode.

○ d. Restart the monitor.

Question 30

> Your company has recently decided to move its Windows 2000 Professional computers to the corporate domain. From the desktop, where would you look to see what workgroup or domain you are currently a member of?
>
> ○ a. Right-click Start, then select Memberships—the information will be displayed on the Identification tab.
>
> ○ b. Right-click the taskbar, then select Memberships—the information will be displayed on the Identification tab.
>
> ○ c. Right-click Network Neighborhood, then select Properties—the information will be displayed on the Identification tab.
>
> ○ d. Right-click My Computer, then select Properties—the information will be displayed on the Identification tab.

Question 31

> You are the lead project manager at your company and you work from a Windows NT 4 workstation. You have been assigned to share certain files from your computer to the network. You are to allow administrators to view your saved work. You have been specifically instructed that administrators are only to be allowed the Read permission and all other groups will have No Access. You share the files and assign the Read permission; however, you are unable to restrict access from other groups. What is the most likely cause of the problem?
>
> ○ a. You cannot assign the Administrators group read-only permissions.
>
> ○ b. The other groups have more privileges than you.
>
> ○ c. The hard drive is formatted FAT-16.
>
> ○ d. You have accidentally assigned yourself No Access to the files.

Question 32

> You are logged on to a Windows NT workstation and you press Ctrl+Alt+Del. What will happen next?
>
> ○ a. The computer will restart.
>
> ○ b. You will be prompted to log in again.
>
> ○ c. You will be asked if you're sure you want to restart the system.
>
> ○ d. The Task Manager will be displayed.

Question 33

To create or delete logical partitions from a Windows NT workstation, which tool should you use?

○ a. Disk Administrator

○ b. FDISK

○ c. Device Manager

○ d. Windows Explorer

Question 34

You have just been to a class on stripe sets and would like to implement them on your home computer that is running Windows 2000 Server. You select your C:, D:, and E: hard drives for your stripe set; however, the stripe set is not created. What is the most likely cause of the problem?

○ a. Stripe sets can have from 2 to 32 disks but not odd numbers of disks.

○ b. Stripe sets will not work on home computers.

○ c. Stripe sets work only on Windows NT 4 servers.

○ d. Stripe sets cannot include the system partition.

Question 35

Of the following, which is the correct RAID level for a stripe set without parity?

○ a. 0

○ b. 1

○ c. 4

○ d. 5

Question 36

You have been assigned to repair a Windows 2000 Professional installation. You have been given an Emergency Repair Disk for the 2000 Professional system. When you attempt to boot the computer from the floppy disk, you receive the error message: "Invalid Media Type: Abort, Retry, Fail". What is the most likely cause of the problem?

○ a. The floppy disk is mislabeled.

○ b. The floppy disk is not formatted with NTFS.

○ c. The hard drive is defective.

○ d. The hard drive is not formatted with NTFS.

Question 37

You have been assigned to reinstall Windows 95 on 30 PCs and to ensure that the existing group items are kept. Beyond reinstalling in the existing Windows directory, what other action should you take to accomplish this task with the least amount of effort?

○ a. Copy the existing groups to floppy disks.

○ b. Make disk images for each of the computers.

○ c. Join the computers to a common workgroup.

○ d. None; the groups will be kept automatically.

Question 38

Your company has been using a Windows 9x computer as a data storage area for documents. Lately, the system has been getting slow because of insufficient disk space. You have been asked to create shares of each of the directories so that the data can be moved to other computers on the network while a larger hard drive is installed. When you return to your workstation, you notice that none of the shares you created are showing up on the network. What is the most likely cause of the problem?

○ a. Insufficient disk space.

○ b. Incompatible network protocols.

○ c. Insufficient permissions to create the shares.

○ d. Shares apply to only the local computer and do not show up on the network.

Question 39

An IP address of 192.xxx.xxx.xxx is which class of IP address?

- ○ a. Class A
- ○ b. Class B
- ○ c. Class C
- ○ d. Class D

Question 40

You are working from a Windows 2000 computer and are unable to browse the network. You suspect that something is wrong with the IP address assigned to you. What command can you run from the command prompt to check your IP address?

- ○ a. **IPCONFIG**
- ○ b. **IPINFO**
- ○ c. **NETSTAT**
- ○ d. **NBTSTAT**

Question 41

Windows 2000 integrates tools to help maintain your system's hard drives. Where would you find the Disk Defragmenter?

- ○ a. My Computer|System|Device Manager|Tools|Disk Defragmenter
- ○ b. My Computer|Hard Drive Properties|Tools|Disk Defragmenter
- ○ c. My Computer|Add New Hardware|Properties|Tools
- ○ d. Start|Programs|Administrative Tools (Common)|Disk Defragmenter

Question 42

A user calls your help line complaining that new software has corrupted a DLL file on their Windows 98 computer. Which of the following can be used to restore the DLL from the original installation disk?

○ a. **RESTORE.COM**

○ b. **REGEDIT32.EXE**

○ c. **CABFIND.EXE**

○ d. **EXTRACT.EXE**

Question 43

You have created a boot disk for troubleshooting and included several DOS utilities; however, you are not able to access CD-ROMs. Which file should you add to your boot disk?

○ a. CDROM.EXE

○ b. MSCDEX.EXE

○ c. MODE.COM

○ d. EDIT.EXE

Question 44

Of the following, which is an example of an email address?

○ a. **http://mail.server.com**

○ b. **name@mail.server.com**

○ c. **ftp://mail.server.com**

○ d. **smtp://name@mail.server.com**

Question 45

Which of the following is the 32-bit command interpreter in Windows NT?

○ a. COMMAND32.EXE

○ b. COMMAND.COM

○ c. CMD32.EXE

○ d. CMD.COM

Question 46

When using Windows 98, which two files are required in the CONFIG.SYS?

○ a. HIMEM.SYS, EMM386.COM

○ b. EMM386.COM, HIMEM.EXE

○ c. EMM386.EXE, HIMEM.COM

○ d. EMM386.EXE, HIMEM.SYS

Question 47

While viewing the Performance tab in Windows 98, you read the message: "Some devices are using MS-DOS compatibility mode". What does this indicate?

○ a. Some devices are not using 32-bit drivers.

○ b. Some devices are accessible only through DOS.

○ c. Some devices have been disabled.

○ d. Some devices must be restarted.

Question 48

You have just enabled file and print sharing on your Windows 98 computer that uses the TCP/IP protocol. Before you're able to share files and printers out on the network, what must you do?

○ a. Create a new account

○ b. Reinstall TCP/IP

○ c. Install a different protocol

○ d. Join the computer to a domain

Question 49

You are trying to copy many files from a single directory in Windows 2000 using Windows Explorer. Which two keys along with your mouse will help simplify the task?

○ a. Ctrl and Tab

○ b. Alt and Ctrl

○ c. Shift and Alt

○ d. Ctrl and Shift

Question 50

In Windows 2000, what is added to an icon in My Computer when a device is shared?

○ a. The word "Shared"

○ b. A picture of a computer

○ c. The word "Available"

○ d. A picture of a hand

Question 51

While installing Windows 98 on a new hard drive, you select No when prompted for large drive support. What will be the maximum size of your primary partition if you continue the installation?

○ a. 4GB

○ b. 2GB

○ c. 0GB; the installation will fail.

○ d. 1GB

Question 52

TCP/IP is an example of which of the following?

- ○ a. A service
- ○ b. A protocol
- ○ c. An adapter
- ○ d. A client

Question 53

Client for Microsoft Networks is an example of which of the following?

- ○ a. A service
- ○ b. A protocol
- ○ c. An adapter
- ○ d. A client

Question 54

File and Print Sharing is an example of which of the following?

- ○ a. A service
- ○ b. A protocol
- ○ c. An adapter
- ○ d. A client

Question 55

Internet Connection Sharing is an example of which of the following?

- ○ a. A service
- ○ b. A protocol
- ○ c. An adapter
- ○ d. A client

Question 56

An Ethernet NIC is an example of which of the following?

○ a. A service

○ b. A protocol

○ c. An adapter

○ d. A client

Question 57

You want to change the logical drive letter of your second hard drive on Windows 2000. Where would you look to find the tool that does this?

○ a. My Computer|Control Panel|Media

○ b. My Computer|Control Panel|Computer Management

○ c. My Computer|Control Panel|Logical Drives

○ d. My Computer|Control Panel|Administrative Tools|Computer Management

Question 58

What is the function of WINS in Windows 2000?

○ a. It is the **startup** command that must be at the end of the AUTOEXEC.BAT.

○ b. It resolves NetBIOS names.

○ c. It is a driver that allows multiboot on NTFS.

○ d. It is the command used to share devices from the command prompt.

Question 59

TCP/IP addresses and subnet masks must be broken down to binary to determine if the address is on the local network or on a remote network. What is the binary equivalent of 255?

○ a. 00000000

○ b. 11110000

○ c. 00001111

○ d. 11111111

Question 60

Your company has decided that the beta version of its customer-management software causes too many problems on the Windows 98 computers and directs you to uninstall it. After uninstalling the software, you get several error messages relating to the Registry. Because you are very familiar with the Registry, you decide to remove all values in the Registry HKeys that relate to the beta software. What should you use to edit the Registry?

○ a. Notepad

○ b. WordPad

○ c. REGEDIT

○ d. Any text editor available

Question 61

File extensions and applications that use OLE in Windows 98 are contained in which Registry HKey?

○ a. HKEY_CLASSES_ROOT

○ b. HKEY_USERS

○ c. HKEY_CURRENT_USER

○ d. HKEY_LOCAL_MACHINE

Question 62

Network information and user configuration options in Windows 98 are contained in which Registry HKey?

○ a. HKEY_CLASSES_ROOT

○ b. HKEY_USERS

○ c. HKEY_CURRENT_USER

○ d. HKEY_LOCAL_MACHINE

Question 63

Information specific to the user configurations at the moment in Windows 98 are contained in which Registry HKey?

○ a. HKEY_CLASSES_ROOT

○ b. HKEY_USERS

○ c. HKEY_CURRENT_USER

○ d. HKEY_LOCAL_MACHINE

Question 64

Information specific to all hardware and software contained on the computer in Windows 98 are contained in which Registry HKey?

○ a. HKEY_CLASSES_ROOT

○ b. HKEY_USERS

○ c. HKEY_CURRENT_USER

○ d. HKEY_LOCAL_MACHINE

Question 65

Information specific to the current hardware profile in Windows 98 is contained in which Registry HKey?

○ a. HKEY_CLASSES_ROOT

○ b. HKEY_USERS

○ c. HKEY_CURRENT_CONFIG

○ d. HKEY_LOCAL_MACHINE

Question 66

Information specific to data in RAM in Windows 98 is contained in which Registry HKey?

○ a. HKEY_CLASSES_ROOT

○ b. HKEY_DYN_DATA

○ c. HKEY_CURRENT_USER

○ d. HKEY_LOCAL_MACHINE

Question 67

One of the primary reasons companies choose Windows NT over Windows 9x is security. Which of the following is an example of a security feature not available in Windows 9x?

○ a. Assign permissions to single files based on group membership.

○ b. Restrict access to Read for folders shared on the network.

○ c. Allow Full Access to files within a share.

○ d. Require a password to access a network share.

Question 68

Windows 2000 has a user interface similar to Windows 9x. Which of the following is an example of an icon found in the Control Panel in Windows 2000 that is not found in Windows 9x?

○ a. Administrative Tools

○ b. Printers

○ c. Keyboard

○ d. Mouse

Question 69

Computer viruses cause considerable damage to companies and individuals. Which of the following best describes a virus that pretends to be a useful program?

○ a. Terminate and Stay Resident (TSR)

○ b. Boot Sector

○ c. Trojan

○ d. Antivirus

Question 70

If you encounter a computer with a boot sector virus, what utility can you use to remove the virus from the hard drive?

○ a. **RDISK/MBR**

○ b. **FDISK/MBR**

○ c. **ERD/MBR**

○ d. **FORMAT/MBR**

A+ OS Technologies
Answer Key #1

1. d	19. c	37. d	55. a
2. d	20. d	38. a	56. c
3. c	21. c	39. c	57. d
4. b	22. b	40. a	58. b
5. b	23. c	41. b	59. d
6. b	24. d	42. d	60. c
7. d	25. b	43. b	61. a
8. c	26. c	44. b	62. b
9. a	27. b	45. d	63. c
10. d	28. b	46. d	64. d
11. c	29. c	47. a	65. c
12. d	30. d	48. d	66. b
13. a	31. c	49. d	67. a
14. a	32. d	50. d	68. a
15. b	33. a	51. b	69. c
16. b	34. d	52. b	70. b
17. d	35. a	53. d	
18. a	36. a	54. a	

Question 1

The correct answer is d. When you place a $ at the end of a share, the share becomes hidden on the network. You can still access the share remotely by using a Universal Naming Convention (UNC). Answers a, b, and c are incorrect because they do not include a $ at the end of the share. Note that the 'InvisibleMan' share in option c will not be accessible by DOS-only machines on the network because of its length.

For more information on this topic, see *A+ Exam Cram, 2nd Edition*, Chapter 12, the section "Windows 9x vs. Windows 3.x".

Question 2

The correct answer is d. Tracert is short for *trace route*. When you run Tracert, the information you receive deals with the path the packets take to reach their destination, the route the packets take, and the time it takes each station to respond. Answer a is incorrect because COMMAND.COM does not have the ability to trace a route as an internal function. Answer b is incorrect because AppleTalk is a network protocol for Macintosh. Answer c is incorrect because Remote Access Service (RAS) is a service that runs in order for you to use Dial Up Networking.

For more information on this topic, see *A+ Exam Cram, 2nd Edition*, Chapter 8, the section "The Internet".

Question 3

The correct answer is c. When you work on a document in Windows 2000, by default the document will by saved in C:\Documents and settings. You can specify another location by selecting Save As from the File menu. Answer a is incorrect because this C:\System32\Temp is where temporary files are kept, not the saved document. Answer b is incorrect because there is no Temp directory off the DeskTop folder. Answer d is incorrect because there is no Documents and files directory off the Program Files directory by default.

For more information on this topic, see *A+ Exam Cram, 2nd Edition*, Chapter 13, the section "Windows 2000".

Question 4

The correct answer is b. When you receive a warning message about files being hidden, and you want to copy them, you must change your view. Windows Explorer will copy only those files that are viewable from the Explorer's view. Answer a is incorrect because Windows Explorer cannot see the files to copy them.

Answer c is incorrect for the same reason a is incorrect; the Windows Explorer cannot see the files. Answer d is incorrect because the Windows Explorer will only put the files where you tell it to.

For more information on this topic, see *A+ Exam Cram, 2nd Edition*, Chapter 12, the section "Windows 98".

Question 5

The correct answer is b. *Folder* is the term that best describes the way Windows allows you to organize files with common themes. Answer a is incorrect because **FORMAT** is a command for formatting disks. Answer c is incorrect because FDISK is a utility used to partition hard disks. Answer d is incorrect because F5 is a function key; on startup of a Windows 9x computer, pressing the F5 key boots the user into Safe Mode.

For more information on this topic, see *A+ Exam Cram, 2nd Edition*, Chapter 10, the section "File Systems".

Question 6

The correct answer is b. When the 512KB limit is reached, the operating system reports insufficient disk space even if you have plenty of free space. Answer a is incorrect because "Invalid command" is the error message you receive when you type an invalid command at the command prompt. Answer c is incorrect because "General Protection Fault in Kernl386.exe" is the error you get when a page fault or memory leak occurs. Answer d is incorrect because "Duplicate file name exists" is the error you get when you try to give a file the same name in the same directory as one that exists there already.

For more information on this topic, see *A+ Exam Cram, 2nd Edition*, Chapter 10, the section "File Systems".

Question 7

The correct answer is d. When you are navigating through the directories on your hard drive and want to return to the root directory of the drive, the command is **CD **. Answer a is incorrect because **CD .** will not take you back at all. Answer b is incorrect because **CD ..** will take you back one level. Answer c is incorrect because there is no **Root** command in DOS.

For more information on this topic, see *A+ Exam Cram, 2nd Edition*, Chapter 10, the section "File Systems".

Question 8

The correct answer is c. The Directory Allocation Table (DAT) is a tracking system used along with the File Allocation Table (FAT). Answer a is incorrect because V-FAT or VFAT (same thing, different notation) is FAT16 and is not "another" system. Answer b is incorrect because there is no such thing as V-DAT. Answer d is incorrect because FAT-32 or FAT32 (same thing, different notation) is a FAT, not "another" system.

For more information on this topic, see *A+ Exam Cram, 2ⁿᵈ Edition*, Chapter 10, the section "File Systems".

Question 9

The correct answer is a. DEFRAG's purpose is to put file clusters in an area where they can be read contiguously; by doing this, the access time, or read time, is enhanced. Answer b is incorrect because the responsibility of organizing files into separate directories is on the user. Answer c is incorrect because DEFRAG does have a DOS-based application available. Answer d is incorrect because Long File Names are stored in the FAT.

For more information on this topic, see *A+ Exam Cram, 2ⁿᵈ Edition*, Chapter 10, the section "DEFRAG.EXE".

Question 10

The correct answer is d. When you issue a search command (**Dir/s**), and you do not give a file extension or wildcard character, most likely you will get a "File Not Found" response. Answers a, b, and c are incorrect because in each case, a file extension is specified.

For more information on this topic, see *A+ Exam Cram, 2ⁿᵈ Edition*, Chapter 10, the section "COMMAND.COM".

Question 11

The correct answer is c. The USB specification for full support is 127 devices, which is accomplished with the use of hubs. Hubs typically hold from 2 to 16 devices. Answer a is incorrect because USBs support many more devices than the standard SCSI controller (which supports seven devices off of the controller). Answers b and d are incorrect because they are made-up answers.

For more information on this topic, see *A+ Exam Cram, 2ⁿᵈ Edition*, Chapter 8, the section "Universal Serial Bus (USB)".

Question 12

The correct answer is d. By definition, a peer-to-peer network consists of equals, all acting as both client and server. Answer a is incorrect because client/server environments have centralized management there is also a server that authenticates the users permissions on the network. Answers b and c are incorrect because any network topology can be used for a network.

For more information on this topic, see *A+ Exam Cram, 2nd Edition*, Chapter 8, the section "Networking Overview".

Question 13

The correct answer is a. IEEE 802.3 defines Ethernet networks. Answer b is incorrect because IEEE 802.5 defines Token ring networks. Answers c and d are incorrect because they are made-up specifications.

For more information on this topic, see *A+ Exam Cram, 2nd Edition*, Chapter 8, the section "Ethernet (IEEE 802.3)".

Question 14

The correct answer is a. From a performance perspective, Microsoft recommends that bus networks not be used with more than 10 workstations. The volume of network traffic may cause the network to provide unacceptable response time with more than 10 workstations. (In reality, however, many networks will run perfectly well beyond 10 workstations.) Answer b is incorrect because 20 workstations may cause performance degradation of the network. Answer c is incorrect because a 50-workstation bus network would be unacceptably slow in many instances. Answer d is incorrect because 100 workstations would be far too many for a bus network. In evaluating topologies, you should examine the intended use of the workstations to verify that the topology will be suitable to the environment.

For more information on this topic, see *A+ Exam Cram, 2nd Edition*, Chapter 8, the section "Network Overview".

Question 15

The correct answer is b. Computers on a single line are considered to be in a bus topology. Answer a is incorrect because ring is the term for forming a logical ring. Answer c is incorrect because star is the term for a network with hubs, branching out in all directions. Answer d is incorrect because a mesh consists of any topologies with many alternate routes (sometimes jokingly referred to as the "mess" topology).

For more information on this topic, see *A+ Exam Cram, 2ⁿᵈ Edition*, Chapter 8, the section "Token Ring".

Question 16

The correct answer is b. The data link layer of the OSI model can be broken into two sublayers, the MAC and the Logical Link Control (LLC) layer. Answer a is incorrect because the Physical layer is "The media"—i.e., "The Wire". Answer c is incorrect because the Network layer is the layer where routing and switching occurs. Answer d is incorrect because the Transport layer is where error recovery occurs; typically, gateways function in this layer.

For more information on this topic, see *A+ Exam Cram, 2ⁿᵈ Edition*, Chapter 8, the section "The OSI Model".

Question 17

The correct answer is d. ISDN uses two channels, each with 64Kbps: 2×64=128. Answer a is incorrect because B-ISDN is 1.5Mbps. Answer b is incorrect because this is a made-up answer. Answer c is incorrect for the same reason b is incorrect, and Kbps has been changed to Mbps, which is much faster than ISDN.

For more information on this topic, see *A+ Exam Cram, 2ⁿᵈ Edition*, Chapter 8, the section "The Internet".

Question 18

The correct answer is a. The **ATTRIB** command is used to set or change the attributes of a file (H=Hidden, R=Read, S=System, A=Archive). Answer b is incorrect because there is no DOS command to prevent the changing of file attributes. Answer c is incorrect because there is no "Ring in Busy" command for modems; it's a made-up answer. Answer d is incorrect because backup programs check for the attributes, but **ATTRIB** is not necessarily the program that set them.

For more information on this topic, see *A+ Exam Cram, 2ⁿᵈ Edition*, Chapter 10, the section "DOS Commands".

Question 19

The correct answer is c. The use of a standard colon is not a valid way to append search criteria to the **Path** statement. Answers a, b, and d are incorrect because each of these will provide a path to the Windows directory. Note that in answer c, the **%path%** is a valid statement and is used for an easier way to visually see in the editor what the path is.

For more information on this topic, see *A+ Exam Cram, 2nd Edition*, Chapter 10, the section "AUTOEXEC.BAT".

Question 20

The correct answer is d. The semicolon is used in INI files to remark out statements. Answers a, b, and c are incorrect because they are made-up answers; no such commands exist.

For more information on this topic, see *A+ Exam Cram, 2nd Edition*, Chapter 11, the section "Initialization (INI) Files".

Question 21

The correct answer is c. The semicolon is a valid mark in INI files. Answers a and b are incorrect because if a command begins with a semicolon in the AUTOEXEC.BAT or CONFIG.SYS file, it will generate an error. Answer b is incorrect for the same reason a is incorrect. Answer d is incorrect because PROGMAN.EXE is not a file you can edit or view by default.

For more information on this topic, see *A+ Exam Cram, 2nd Edition*, Chapter 11, the section "Initialization (INI) Files".

Question 22

The correct answer is b. A floppy drive cannot be formatted with NTFS; the file system takes up more than the space available on a floppy. Answer a is incorrect because hard drives can be formatted with NTFS. Answer c is incorrect because a strip set can be formatted with NTFS. Answer d is incorrect because a volume set can be formatted with NTFS.

For more information on this topic, see *A+ Exam Cram, 2nd Edition*, Chapter 13, the section "NT File System (NTFS)".

Question 23

The correct answer is c. NTFS is not a supported File System of Windows 98; therefore, when you have an NTFS drive on the system, it does not show up, and Drive Converter can not operate on it. Answers a and b are incorrect because

FAT-16 or VFAT can be converted. Answer d is incorrect because blank partitions can be converted to FAT-32.

For more information on this topic, see *A+ Exam Cram, 2nd Edition*, Chapter 13, the section "NT Workstation and NT Server".

Question 24

The correct answer is d. The "No operating system" error message is the result of no IO.SYS file being found; when you run the **SYS** command, the system files are transferred and the system can boot. Answer a is incorrect because reformatting the hard drive will make the problem worse. Answer b is incorrect because reinstalling DOS will take more effort than running the **SYS** command. Answer c is incorrect because repartitioning the hard drive will erase all data.

For more information on this topic, see *A+ Exam Cram, 2nd Edition*, Chapter 11, the section "Booting and System Files".

Question 25

The correct answer is b. Many of the utilities found in Windows 9x are also in Windows 2000; the Device Manager is very similar and the symbols are the same for Windows 2000 as they are in Windows 9x. Answer a is incorrect because a red x is the symbol for a device that has been found but has conflicts. Answers c and d are incorrect; there are no such symbols in Device Manager.

For more information on this topic, see *A+ Exam Cram, 2nd Edition*, Chapter 13, the section "Windows 2000 Diagnostics and Troubleshooting".

Question 26

The correct answer is c. DEFRAG places files in contiguous areas on your hard drive, making access faster. Answer a is incorrect because REGEDIT is for editing the Registry. Answer b is incorrect because MEMMAKER is for better utilizing RAM, not hard drive space. Answer d is incorrect because CHKDISK (Check Disk) is incorrect because it only reports the status of the drive and finds lost files and clusters.

For more information on this topic, see *A+ Exam Cram, 2nd Edition*, Chapter 12, the section "Reports and Utilities".

Question 27

The correct answer is b. Event Viewer is the tool used to view the errors encountered while starting Windows NT. Answer a is incorrect because the CMOS is for setting initial values. Answer c is incorrect because the Task Manager is for viewing and manipulating running services. Answer d is incorrect because the CONFIG.SYS file is for specifying device drivers; it does not report problems.

For more information on this topic, see *A+ Exam Cram, 2nd Edition*, Chapter 13, the section "Troubleshooting Tools".

Question 28

The correct answer is b. An incremental backup backs up only the files that have changed since the last backup. Answer a is incorrect because a differential backup backs up files that have been added since the last backup. Answer c is incorrect because a full backup backs up all files. Answer d is incorrect because there is no such thing as a mixed-mode backup.

For more information on this topic, see *A+ Exam Cram, 2nd Edition*, Chapter 12, the section "Reports and Utilities".

Question 29

The correct answer is c. Safe Mode by default will start in 640×480 display mode because only standard VGA is used in Safe Mode. Answer a is incorrect because reinstalling the video adapter driver takes more effort than restarting in Safe Mode. Answer b is incorrect for the same reason a is incorrect; reinstalling takes more effort than restarting. Answer d is incorrect because restarting the monitor does nothing for the resolution settings of the video driver.

For more information on this topic, see *A+ Exam Cram, 2nd Edition*, Chapter 13, the section "Windows 2000".

Question 30

The correct answer is d. In Windows 2000, the computer identification is located in the properties of My Computer. Answer a is incorrect because the Start button does not contain information about the workgroup or domain. Answer b is incorrect because the taskbar has only information about tasks running and the taskbar's settings. Answer c is incorrect because there is no Network Neighborhood icon in Windows 2000.

For more information on this topic, see *A+ Exam Cram, 2nd Edition*, Chapter 13, the section "Windows 2000 Diagnostics and Troubleshooting".

Question 31

The correct answer is c. When a hard drive is formatted FAT-16, the NTFS options are not available. Answer a is incorrect because you can assign any group any permission. Answer b is incorrect because the scenario states that the other groups have No Access. Answer d is incorrect because you had the ability to change the attribute of the file.

For more information on this topic, see *A+ Exam Cram, 2nd Edition*, Chapter 13, the section "NT File System (NTFS)".

Question 32

The correct answer is d. When you press Ctrl+Alt+Del on an NT system after being logged in, the Task Manager is brought to the forefront. Answer a is incorrect because this key combination causes the computer to restart on a DOS-based system. Answer b is incorrect because the Task Manager will not ask you to log in again; however, you will have the option of logging off. Answer c is incorrect because the Task Manager presents options for you when you press Ctrl+Alt+Del; it does not ask you if you want to restart the system.

For more information on this topic, see *A+ Exam Cram, 2nd Edition*, Chapter 13, the section "Troubleshooting Tools".

Question 33

The correct answer is a. Disk Administrator is the tool used to change, create, or modify partitions in Windows NT. Answer b is incorrect because FDISK is not an NT GUI application. Answer c is incorrect because the Device Manager is used to check the status of a device. Answer d is incorrect because Windows Explorer is used to view the contents of drives and properties of files, not to modify partitions.

For more information on this topic, see *A+ Exam Cram, 2nd Edition*, Chapter 13, the section "NT Disk Administration".

Question 34

The correct answer is d. Stripe sets cannot include the system partition. Answer a is incorrect because stripe sets can have odd numbers of disks; the only requirement is that you cannot have the system partition, and all drives or partitions striped must be the same size. Answer b is incorrect because stripe sets can be used on home computers. Answer c is incorrect because stripe sets will work with all NT 4 and Windows 2000 operating systems.

For more information on this topic, see *A+ Exam Cram, 2nd Edition*, Chapter 13, the section "NT Disk Administration".

Question 35

The correct answer is a. Stripe sets without parity are RAID level 0 because they provide no fault tolerance. Answer b is incorrect because RAID level 1 is disk mirroring. Answer c is incorrect because RAID level 3 is stripe set with parity. Answer d is incorrect because RAID level 5 is the most fault tolerant.

For more information on this topic, see *A+ Exam Cram, 2nd Edition*, Chapter 13, the section "NT Disk Administration".

Question 36

The correct answer is a. The most likely cause from the choices given is that the disk is mislabeled. Answer b is incorrect because the overhead required of NTFS will not fit on a floppy disk. Answer c is incorrect because the error occurs when you use the floppy to attempt to boot. Answer d is incorrect because NT will install and run on a hard drive that is formatted FAT-16.

For more information on this topic, see *A+ Exam Cram, 2nd Edition*, Chapter 14, the section "Startup Problems".

Question 37

The correct answer is d. When you reinstall Windows 95 in the same directory as it was originally installed, the groups are automatically kept. Answer a is incorrect because copying the existing groups to floppy disks will take more effort than just reinstalling. Answer b is incorrect for the same reason answer a is incorrect; making disk images for each of the computers takes more effort than just reinstalling. Answer c is incorrect because workgroup memberships do not affect the group files on the local computer when reinstalling—this is because you will not be on the network during the reinstall.

For more information on this topic, see *A+ Exam Cram, 2nd Edition*, Chapter 12, the section "Installing Windows 95, 98, and ME".

Question 38

The correct answer is a. When a Windows 9x computer runs low on disk space, one of the symptoms is that shares do not show up on the network. Answer b is incorrect because you could not have used the machine as a data-sharing point if the protocols where incompatible. Answer c is incorrect because the scenario states you created the shares, so you had the permission. Answer d is incorrect because shares are for the network; the local computer can access the files directly.

For more information on this topic, see *A+ Exam Cram, 2nd Edition*, Chapter 12, the section "Windows 9x vs. Windows 3.x".

Question 39

The correct answer is c. A Class C network address begins with 192 through 223 for the first octet. Answer a is incorrect because a Class A address begins with 1 through 126. Answer b is incorrect because a Class B address begins with 128 through 191. Answer d is incorrect because a Class D address begins with 224 through 239.

For more information on this topic, see *A+ Exam Cram, 2nd Edition*, Chapter 8, the section "Bridges and Routers".

Question 40

The correct answer is a. **IPCONFIG** displays the basic information associated with your IP configuration. Answer b is incorrect because there is no **IPINFO** command. Answer c is incorrect because **NETSTAT** displays the active TCP connections. Answer d is incorrect because **NBTSTAT** displays NetBIOS information.

For more information on this topic, see *A+ Exam Cram, 2nd Edition*, Chapter 13, the section "Windows 2000".

Question 41

The correct answer is b. The Disk Defragmenter can be accessed by going through My Computer, then selecting a hard drive and displaying its properties, then clicking the Tools tab and selecting Defragment Now. Answer a is incorrect because there is no Tools tab from the Device Manager. Answer c is incorrect because there is no Properties option once inside Add New Hardware. Answer d is incorrect because there is no Administrative Tools (Common) option from the Program menu in Windows 2000.

For more information on this topic, see *A+ Exam Cram, 2nd Edition*, Chapter 14, the section "Diagnostics Tools".

Question 42

The correct answer is d. EXTRACT is the utility that extracts DLL files from the original CAB files. Answer a is incorrect because **RESTORE** is not a valid command in Windows 98. Answer b is incorrect because **REGEDIT32** is for Registry editing. Answer c is incorrect because **CABFIND** is not a valid command in Windows 98.

For more information on this topic, see *A+ Exam Cram, 2nd Edition*, Chapter 12, the section "Installation Phases".

Question 43

The correct answer is b. MSCDEX is the utility included with Microsoft operating systems that allows CD-ROM support. Answer a is incorrect because CDROM.EXE is not a valid utility. Answer c is incorrect because MODE is used for redirecting print functions. Answer d is incorrect because EDIT is for editing files.

For more information on this topic, see *A+ Exam Cram, 2nd Edition*, Chapter 12, the section "Installing Windows 95, 98, and ME".

Question 44

The correct answer is b. An email address consists of a username and a mail service name. Answer a is incorrect because this is an example of a Web page. Answer c is incorrect because this is an example of an FTP site address. Answer d is incorrect because SMTP is neither a site nor an address; it is a protocol.

For more information on this topic, see *A+ Exam Cram, 2nd Edition*, Chapter 8, the section "The Internet".

Question 45

The correct answer is d. CMD.COM is the 32-bit command interpreter in Windows NT. Answer a is incorrect because there is no such file in Windows NT. Answer b is incorrect because COMMAND.COM is the 16-bit command interpreter in Windows NT. Answer c is incorrect because there is no such file in Windows NT.

For more information on this topic, see *A+ Exam Cram, 2nd Edition*, Chapter 13, the section "NT Workstation and NT Server".

Question 46

The correct answer is d. EMM386.EXE and HIMEM.SYS are required in the CONFIG.SYS for Windows 98 to give access to the high memory and extended memory. Answer a is incorrect because there is no such file as EMM386.COM. Answer b is incorrect because there is no such file as HIMEM.EXE. Answer c is incorrect because there is no such file as HIMEM.COM.

For more information on this topic, see *A+ Exam Cram, 2ⁿᵈ Edition*, Chapter 12, the section "Starting Windows 9x".

Question 47

The correct answer is a. When a device does not have a 32-bit driver but is still accessible to the Windows 9x operating system, it will display the message: "Some devices are using MS-DOS compatibility mode". Answer b is incorrect because the device is accessible through Windows. Answer c is incorrect because you view disabled devices through the Device Manager. Answer d is incorrect because there is no indicator in the Performance tab to inform you when a device attached to the system must be restarted.

For more information on this topic, see *A+ Exam Cram, 2ⁿᵈ Edition*, Chapter 12, the section "Windows 9x vs. Windows 3.x".

Question 48

The correct answer is d. When you share resources from a computer, you are doing it to be able to give others access. You are able to access resources on the local machine without having to share them; in order to give others access, you must be on a network. Answer a is incorrect because you created the share; a new account is not necessary. Answer b is incorrect because it is not necessary to reinstall TCP/IP when you create shares. Answer c is incorrect because TCP/IP allows sharing of files and printers.

For more information on this topic, see *A+ Exam Cram, 2ⁿᵈ Edition*, Chapter 8, the section "Networking Overview".

Question 49

The correct answer is d. The Ctrl and the Shift keys both help while copying multiple files; pressing the Shift key and clicking selects all files from the start point to the end point, and pressing the Ctrl key selects each file you click. Answer a is incorrect because the Tab key has no special function for copying files. Answers b and c are incorrect because the Alt key is for moving individual files.

For more information on this topic, see *A+ Exam Cram, 2ⁿᵈ Edition*, Chapter 12, the section "Windows 9x vs. Windows 3.x".

Question 50

The correct answer is d. When a folder is shared, a picture of a hand is added to the icon. Answer a is incorrect because the word "Shared" is not added. Answer b is incorrect because there is no such symbol for sharing. Answer c is incorrect because the word "Available" is not added.

For more information on this topic, see *A+ Exam Cram, 2ⁿᵈ Edition*, Chapter 12, the section "Windows 9x vs. Windows 3.x".

Question 51

The correct answer is b. The large drive support option that is presented when you install Windows 98 appears only if you have a hard drive larger than 2GB and LBA support. If you choose Yes, then you will have the option of making the entire hard drive the primary partition. Answer a is incorrect because without large drive support, the 2GB limit of FAT-16 is the maximum size available. Answer c is incorrect because the installation will work. Answer d is incorrect because the maximum size is 2GB.

For more information on this topic, see *A+ Exam Cram, 2ⁿᵈ Edition*, Chapter 12, the section "FAT32".

Question 52

The correct answer is b. TCP/IP is a protocol. Answer a is incorrect because a service works with protocols. Answer c is incorrect because an adapter works with protocols. Answer d is incorrect because a client works with protocols.

For more information on this topic, see *A+ Exam Cram, 2ⁿᵈ Edition*, Chapter 8, the section "Networking Overview".

Question 53

The correct answer is d. Client for Microsoft networks is an example of an installable client. Answer a is incorrect because a service deals with files and devices. Answer b is incorrect because a protocol is a communication standard. Answer c is incorrect because an adapter is the device drive for the physical network interface card (NIC).

For more information on this topic, see *A+ Exam Cram, 2nd Edition*, Chapter 8, the section "Networking Overview".

Question 54

The correct answer is a. Services deal with files and device sharing. Answer b is incorrect because a protocol is a communication standard. Answer c is incorrect because an adapter is the device driver for the physical NIC. Answer d is incorrect because a client is software that deals with the type of network you are on.

For more information on this topic, see *A+ Exam Cram, 2nd Edition*, Chapter 8, the section "Networking Overview".

Question 55

The correct answer is a. Services deal with files and device sharing. Answer b is incorrect because a protocol is a communication standard. Answer c is incorrect because an adapter is the device driver for the physical NIC. Answer d is incorrect because a client is software that deals with the type of network you are on.

For more information on this topic, see *A+ Exam Cram, 2nd Edition*, Chapter 8, the section "Networking Overview".

Question 56

The correct answer is c. An adapter is the device driver for the physical NIC. Answer a is incorrect because services deal with files and device sharing. Answer b is incorrect because a protocol is a communication standard. Answer d is incorrect because a client is software that deals with the type of network you are on.

For more information on this topic, see *A+ Exam Cram, 2nd Edition*, Chapter 8, the section "Networking Overview".

Question 57

The correct answer is d. The Disk Administrator is located in Computer Management in Windows 2000. When accessing this tool from My Computer, you must go through the Administrative Tools icon. Answer a is incorrect because the Media icon grants access to the sound devices. Answer b is incorrect because you must go through the Administrative Tools icon. Answer c is incorrect because there is no Logical Drives icon.

For more information on this topic, see *A+ Exam Cram, 2nd Edition*, Chapter 14, the section "Diagnostics Tools".

Question 58

The correct answer is b. The function of WINS is to resolve NetBIOS names. Answer a is incorrect because the command to start Windows in the AUTOEXEC.BAT is **WIN**. Answer c is incorrect because there is no multiboot driver for Windows 2000. Answer d is incorrect because the command to share devices from the command prompt is **NET**.

For more information on this topic, see *A+ Exam Cram, 2nd Edition*, Chapter 13, the section "NT Networking".

Question 59

The correct answer is d. 255 in binary is represented as eight 1s. Answer a is incorrect because all 0s represents 0. Answer b is incorrect because four 1s and four 0s represents 240. Answer c is incorrect because four 0s and four 1s represents 15.

For more information on this topic, see *A+ Exam Cram, 2nd Edition*, Chapter 5, the section "Interrupt Requests (IRQs)".

Question 60

The correct answer is c. REGEDIT is the utility for editing the Registry, because the Registry is a binary file and cannot be edited with standard text editors. Answer a is incorrect because Notepad is a text editor. Answer b is incorrect because WordPad is a text editor. Answer d is incorrect for the same reason a and b are incorrect; you cannot use a text editor on a binary file.

For more information on this topic, see *A+ Exam Cram, 2nd Edition*, Chapter 12, the section "The Registry".

Question 61

The correct answer is a. The HKEY_CLASSES_ROOT deals with Object Link Embedding (OLE) programs. Answer b is incorrect because HKEY_USERS deals with network and user options. Answer c is incorrect because

HKEY_CURRENT_USER deals with the user logged on at the moment. Answer d is incorrect because HKEY_LOCAL_MACHINE deals with the hardware and software on the local machine.

For more information on this topic, see *A+ Exam Cram, 2nd Edition*, Chapter 12, the section "The Registry".

Question 62

The correct answer is b. The HKEY_USERS key deals with network and user configurations. Answer a is incorrect because HKEY_CLASSES_ROOT deals with the OLE settings. Answer c is incorrect because HKEY_CURRENT_USER deals with the user logged on at the moment. Answer d is incorrect because HKEY_LOCAL_MACHINE deals with hardware and software on the local machine.

For more information on this topic, see *A+ Exam Cram, 2nd Edition*, Chapter 12, the section "The Registry".

Question 63

The correct answer is c. The HKEY_CURRENT_USER key deals with the user logged on at the moment. Answer a is incorrect because HKEY_CLASSES_ROOT deals with OLE. Answer b is incorrect because HKEY_USERS deals with network and user options. Answer d is incorrect because HKEY_LOCAL_MACHINE deals with the hardware and software on the local machine.

For more information on this topic, see *A+ Exam Cram, 2nd Edition*, Chapter 12, the section "The Registry".

Question 64

The correct answer is d. The HKEY_LOCAL_MACHINE key deals with the local machine, software, and hardware; this key is not specific to the user's profile logged on at the moment. Answer a is incorrect because HKEY_CLASSES_ROOT deals with OLE. Answer b is incorrect because HKEY_USERS deals with network and user options. Answer c is incorrect because HKEY_CURRENT_USER deals with the user logged on at the moment.

For more information on this topic, see *A+ Exam Cram, 2nd Edition*, Chapter 12, the section "The Registry".

Question 65

The correct answer is c. The HKEY_CURRENT_CONFIG is specific to the current user. Answer a is incorrect because HKEY_CLASSES_ROOT deals with OLE. Answer b is incorrect because HKEY_USERS deals with network and user options. Answer d is incorrect because HKEY_LOCAL_MACHINE deals with the software and hardware installed on the machine.

For more information on this topic, see *A+ Exam Cram, 2nd Edition*, Chapter 12, the section "The Registry".

Question 66

The correct answer is b. HKEY_DYN_DATA keeps track of how dynamic data is used. Answer a is incorrect because HKEY_CLASSES_ROOT deals with OLE. Answer c is incorrect because HKEY_CURRENT_USER deals with the current profile. Answer d is incorrect because HKEY_LOCAL_MACHINE deals with machine-specific hardware and software.

For more information on this topic, see *A+ Exam Cram, 2nd Edition*, Chapter 12, the section "The Registry".

Question 67

The correct answer is a. The Windows NT operating system allows much more security than the Windows 9x family. The ability to assign permissions based on group membership is unique in the Windows family; only NT versions allow this option. Answer b is incorrect because all versions of Windows allow you to assign Read, even if it is nothing more than an attribute. Answer c is incorrect because this is the default state of a shared file; by default everyone has Full Access when you share a file. Answer d is incorrect because Windows allows user-level and share-level access to folders.

For more information on this topic, see *A+ Exam Cram, 2nd Edition*, Chapter 13, the section "NT Workstation and NT Server".

Question 68

The correct answer is a. Administrative Tools is commonly found in Microsoft NT versions of Windows and Windows 2000, but not Windows 9x. Answers b, c, and d are incorrect because the Printers, Keyboard, and Mouse icons are common in all varieties of Windows.

For more information on this topic, see *A+ Exam Cram, 2ⁿᵈ Edition*, Chapter 13, the section "The Origins of Windows NT".

Question 69

The correct answer is c. A Trojan is a virus that masquerades as another type of program; the name comes from the story of the Trojan Horse. Answer a is incorrect because a TSR is a specific type of application. The Trojan program could be a TSR; however, the question asks for the best definition. Answer b is incorrect for the same reason a is incorrect; it is not the best definition. Answer d is incorrect because an antivirus program is a tool used to get rid of a virus.

For more information on this topic, see *A+ Exam Cram, 2ⁿᵈ Edition*, Chapter 14, the section "Viruses".

Question 70

The correct answer is b. **FDISK/MBR** partitions the hard drive and wipes the Master Boot Record (MBR) clean; this will eliminate a boot sector virus. Answer a is incorrect because **RDISK** is the command for creating an Emergency Repair Disk on Windows NT, and **/MBR** is not a valid switch. Answer c is incorrect because ERD is not a command; it stands for Emergency Repair Disk. Answer d is incorrect because there is no **/MBR** option in **FORMAT**.

For more information on this topic, see *A+ Exam Cram, 2ⁿᵈ Edition*, Chapter 14, the section "Viruses".

A+ OS Technologies Practice Test #2

Question 1

During the boot up of a Windows 98 computer, what is the correct booting sequence?

- ○ a. BIOS initialization, Real Mode MS-DOS driver loading, Real Mode VxD Loader, Protected Mode operating system initialization

- ○ b. Real Mode MS-DOS driver loading, BIOS initialization, Real Mode VxD Loader, Protected Mode operating system initialization

- ○ c. BIOS initialization, Real Mode VxD Loader, Real Mode MS-DOS driver loading, Protected Mode operating system initialization

- ○ d. BIOS initialization, Protected Mode operating system initialization, Real Mode VxD Loader, Real Mode MS-DOS driver loading

Question 2

During the boot up of a DOS-based system, what is the correct boot sequence?

- ○ a. COMMAND.COM, CONFIG.SYS, AUTOEXEC.BAT, IO.SYS, MSDOS.SYS

- ○ b. IO.SYS, MSDOS.SYS, CONFIG.SYS, COMMAND.COM, AUTOEXEC.BAT

- ○ c. CONFIG.SYS, COMMAND.COM, MSDOS.SYS, AUTOEXEC.BAT, IO.SYS

- ○ d. AUTOEXEC.BAT, COMMAND.COM, CONFIG.SYS, IO.SYS, MSDOS.SYS

Question 3

Which of the following options of EMM386.EXE excludes a memory address for loading device drivers?

○ a. Device C:\DOS\EMM386.EXE /NoEMS

○ b. Device C:\DOS\EMM386.EXE NOEMS

○ c. Device C:\DOS\EMM386.EXE X=C800-C9FF

○ d. Device C:\DOS\EMM386.EXE E=C800-C9FF

Question 4

The File Allocation Table (FAT) that is commonly used on floppy drives is which of the following?

○ a. FAT-32

○ b. FAT-16

○ c. FAT-24

○ d. FAT-12

Question 5

When using the FDISK utility, which of the following statements are true?

○ a. The active partition is always labeled C:.

○ b. The primary partition must be labeled C:.

○ c. The maximum number of extended partitions you can create is 26, one for each letter of the alphabet.

○ d. The FDISK utility can also be used to create partitions on floppy disks.

Question 6

Which of the following files are the minimum files required to make a floppy disk bootable?

- ○ a. MSDOS.SYS, IO.SYS, COMMAND.COM
- ○ b. MSDOS.SYS, COMMAND.COM, AUTOEXEC.BAT
- ○ c. IO.SYS, AUTOEXEC.BAT, CONFIG.SYS
- ○ d. COMMAND.COM, CONFIG.SYS, IO.SYS

Question 7

Which of the following is a valid DOS (FAT-16) file name?

- ○ a. %path%.cfg
- ○ b. R+B.exe
- ○ c. MYDOC.$1
- ○ d. Study.txt

Question 8

The Windows 9x operating system contains which three primary files?

- ○ a. WIN.INI, SYSTEM.INI, REGEDIT.EXE
- ○ b. USER.EXE, GDI.EXE, KRNL386.EXE
- ○ c. CONFIG.SYS, IO.SYS, MSDOS.SYS
- ○ d. NTLDR.EXE, SYSTEM.EXE, WIN.COM

Question 9

When you type "Sysedit" in the Run line of a Windows 98 computer, which files will be opened for editing when you execute the command?

- ○ a. SYSTEM.INI, WIN.INI, PROGMAN.INI, CONTROL.INI
- ○ b. AUTOEXEC.BAT, WIN.INI, CONFIG.SYS, SYSTEM.INI
- ○ c. WIN.INI, SYSTEM.INI, CONFIG.SYS, PROGMAN.INI
- ○ d. PROGMAN.INI, SYSTEM.INI, CONFIG.SYS, AUTOEXEC.BAT

Question 10

Windows uses swap files to simulate Random Access Memory (RAM). If you viewed the file name 386SPART.PAR in Windows Explorer, what type of swap file would you have?

○ a. A temporary swap file.

○ b. A corrupted swap file.

○ c. A permanent swap file.

○ d. The existence of the SPART.PAR file means there is no swap file.

Question 11

When using the TCP/IP protocol with Windows 9x configured to automatically obtain an IP address, what type of service is required on the network for the computer to obtain its TCP/IP address?

○ a. A Dynamic Host Configuration Protocol (DHCP) Server

○ b. A Domain Name Server (DNS)

○ c. A Windows Internet Name Server (WINS)

○ d. A Post Office Protocol 3 (POP3) Server

Question 12

When using share-level security on a Windows 9x system, which of the following is true of a shared folder?

○ a. Everyone in the network has full access permissions.

○ b. Only systems administrators can access the shared folder.

○ c. You must enter a password to gain access to the share.

○ d. A domain controller will automatically check to see if you have access to the share.

Question 13

Windows 9x supports Long File Names (LFNs). If you save a file named "Im going to pass this test.txt" what 8.3 file name would you see from DOS?

- ○ a. Im~1.txt
- ○ b. Imgoin~1.txt
- ○ c. Im goin~1.txt
- ○ d. ~Imgoing.txt

Question 14

In Windows 9x, a Registry was added to help simplify and streamline configuration issues. Which two files comprise the Windows 9x Registry?

- ○ a. AUTOEXEC.BAT, CONFIG.SYS
- ○ b. REGEDIT.EXE, REG.SYS
- ○ c. USER.EXE, SYSTEM.INI
- ○ d. SYSTEM.DAT, USER.DAT

Question 15

A customer has called your help line saying that she is unable to create a new directory on her computer. You discover through questioning that the customer has a 40GB hard drive with 20GB free. You ask the customer to read you a list of the files and directories on the root drive of the system and discover there are several LFNs, and that in fact there is still 20GB of hard disk space available. What is the most likely reason the customer cannot create a new directory on the hard drive?

- ○ a. The system is incorrectly reporting the amount of available hard drive space.
- ○ b. The directory the customer is trying to create is not the same size as the other directories.
- ○ c. The Windows 9x operating system limit of 512 directories has been reached because of the LFNs.
- ○ d. The Windows 9x operating system does not allow you to create directories off of the root directory.

Question 16

A customer has called your help line saying that he is no longer able to access DOS since adding Windows 9x to his system. What key(s) should you tell the customer to press during boot up?

○ a. Ctrl+Alt+Del

○ b. F8

○ c. F4

○ d. F5

Question 17

Which file is most likely missing from the system if you receive the following error on boot up: "Bad or missing command interpreter"?

○ a. IO.SYS

○ b. MSDOS.SYS

○ c. COMMAND.COM

○ d. WIN.COM

Question 18

Where on a Windows 95 computer would you look to enable user-level security?

○ a. In the Network Properties under the Access Control tab.

○ b. In the Internet Explorer Properties under the Connections tab.

○ c. In the Control Panel under the Users And Groups icon.

○ d. Right-click the Start button and select User Level Security.

Question 19

Which of the following disk formats is unreadable by a Windows 9x operating system?

○ a. FAT-12

○ b. FAT-32

○ c. FAT-16

○ d. NTFS

Question 20

Which of the following disk formats is unreadable by a Windows NT 4 operating system?

○ a. FAT-12

○ b. FAT-32

○ c. FAT-16

○ d. NTFS

Question 21

Which of the following disk formats is readable by a Windows 2000 operating system but was unsupported in Windows NT 4?

○ a. FAT-12

○ b. FAT-32

○ c. FAT-16

○ d. NTFS

Question 22

When installing Windows 2000 from DOS, which of the following commands would you type at the command prompt?

- ○ a. **WINNT.EXE**
- ○ b. **WINNT32.EXE**
- ○ c. **WIN2K.EXE**
- ○ d. **SETUP.EXE**

Question 23

When installing a Windows 2000 operating system to create a dual boot from Windows 98, what command should you run?

- ○ a. **WINNT.EXE**
- ○ b. **WINNT32.EXE**
- ○ c. **WIN2K.EXE**
- ○ d. **SETUP.EXE**

Question 24

When installing a Windows 98 operating system on a computer that only uses MS-DOS 6.22, what command should you run?

- ○ a. **WIN98.EXE**
- ○ b. **WIN.EXE**
- ○ c. **WINME.EXE**
- ○ d. **SETUP.EXE**

Question 25

When a device has been disabled on a Windows 9x operating system, what is the symbol shown in the Device Manager?

- ○ a. A yellow circle with a black exclamation point
- ○ b. A red X
- ○ c. A yellow circle with a red exclamation point
- ○ d. A black X

Question 26

What is the term that describes the process of calling 16-bit programs into 32-bit programs?

- ○ a. Thunking
- ○ b. Thrashing
- ○ c. Corrupting
- ○ d. Truncating

Question 27

You have two desktop applications running and one fails. You need to save the data from the running application. Which procedure has the best chance of allowing you to save your data from the running application?

- ○ a. Wait a few moments to see if the application not responding will terminate. If not, open the Task Manager and end the task that is not responding, then save your data and reboot the computer.
- ○ b. Wait a few moments to see if the application not responding will terminate. If not, press the reset button on the computer; the application will automatically save the information for you.
- ○ c. Open the Task Manager immediately and chose End Task on the running application. During the shutdown of the application, you will be prompted to save your data.
- ○ d. Immediately click the Start button and select Shut Down. The Task Manager will end the program not responding, and during shutdown you will be prompted to save your data.

Question 28

In which file would you most likely see the command **Prompt=PG**?

○ a. CONFIG.SYS

○ b. WIN.INI

○ c. SYSTEM.INI

○ d. AUTOEXEC.BAT

Question 29

In the Windows 95 operating system, the virtual machine (VM) provides shared memory address space for which of the following?

○ a. All 32-bit applications

○ b. All Windows-based applications

○ c. All applications

○ d. All Internet-aware utilities

Question 30

Windows 95 provides advanced troubleshooting options for dealing with a variety of problems. If you are experiencing a problem with a hard drive that is not fully compatible with Windows 95, which of the following advanced troubleshooting options should you select?

○ a. Disable file sharing

○ b. Disable write behind caching

○ c. Disable Long File Names

○ d. Disable all 32-bit Protected Mode disk drivers

Question 31

When a 32-bit application on a Windows 98 system fails to respond, what applications are affected?

- ○ a. All 16-bit and 32-bit applications
- ○ b. All 32-bit applications
- ○ c. All 16-bit applications
- ○ d. Only the application that failed to respond

Question 32

When installing or upgrading Windows 9x on a network, what three things must you supply?

- ○ a. Username, Computer Name, Workgroup
- ○ b. Username, Computer Name, Domain Name Server
- ○ c. Username, Computer Name, Internet Information Server
- ○ d. Username, Computer Name, Dynamic Host Configuration Server

Question 33

Which of the following icons are not found in the Windows 95 Control Panel?

- ○ a. Network Neighborhood
- ○ b. Dial-Up Networking
- ○ c. Modems
- ○ d. Add/Remove Programs

Question 34

On Windows 9x computers, a yellow circle with a black exclamation point next to a device in the Device Manager means which of the following?

○ a. The device does not have the correct driver installed.

○ b. The device requires you to restart your computer in order to finish installing it.

○ c. The device is detected but has conflicts.

○ d. The device is not compatible with Windows 9x.

Question 35

When you first open Windows Explorer on Windows 2000 computers after a default installation, what file types are hidden?

○ a. INI, DLL, INF

○ b. INI, DLL, VXD

○ c. INI, DLL, BAT

○ d. INI, DLL, EXE

Question 36

ScanDisk is a Windows utility designed to find and repair problems with which types of media?

○ a. CD-RWs and CD-Rs

○ b. Floppy disks and hard drives

○ c. Zip disks and DVDs

○ d. Floppy disks and CD-RWs

Question 37

MS-DOS can be broken down into two types of commands: internal and external. Of the following, which command is an internal command?

- ○ a. **EDIT**
- ○ b. **XCOPY**
- ○ c. **DIR**
- ○ d. **DELTREE**

Question 38

MS-DOS can be broken down into two types of commands, internal and external. Of the following, which command is an external command?

- ○ a. **DIR**
- ○ b. **MD**
- ○ c. **SET**
- ○ d. **XCOPY**

Question 39

Commands that are internal in DOS reside inside the command interpreter. Which of the following files is the DOS command interpreter?

- ○ a. IO.SYS
- ○ b. MSDOS.SYS
- ○ c. COMMAND.COM
- ○ d. EDIT.EXE

Question 40

By default, when is the Windows NT Administrator account created?

○ a. During installation.

○ b. After joining a domain.

○ c. After installing an NT server in the local network.

○ d. For security, the NT Administrator account is only created by default after you register your domain.

Question 41

Windows 2000 integrates tools to help maintain your system's hard drives. Where would you find the Disk Defragmenter?

○ a. My Computer|System|Device Manager|Tools|Disk Defragmenter

○ b. My Computer|right-click on *Hard Drive*|Properties| Tools|Defragment Now

○ c. My Computer|Add New Hardware|Properties|Tools

○ d. Start|Programs|Administrative Tools (Common)|Disk Defragmenter

Question 42

Windows 98 integrates tools to help maintain your system's hard drives. Where would you find the Disk Defragmenter?

○ a. My Computer|Disk Defragmenter

○ b. My Computer|Tools|Disk Defragmenter

○ c. My Computer|right-click on *Hard Drive*|Properties|Tools|Disk Defragmenter

○ d. My Computer|right-click on *Hard Drive*|Properties|Advanced|Disk Defragmenter

Question 43

In Windows 9x, NT 4, and 2000, how do you access the Properties option for a hard drive in My Computer?

○ a. Double-click the Hard Drive icon and select Properties.

○ b. Double-click the Properties icon and select from there.

○ c. Right-click the Hard Drive icon and select Properties.

○ d. Right-click the Properties icon and select the hard drive.

Question 44

Currently you are running Windows 98 and you want to add Windows NT 4. When you create the multiboot, what DOS file gets modified?

○ a. COMMAND.COM

○ b. IO.SYS

○ c. MSDOS.SYS

○ d. BOOT.INI

Question 45

The boot sequence of a computer running Windows 9x should be which of the following?

○ a. BIOS, POST, Boot Sector, GUI

○ b. GUI, POST, BIOS, Boot Sector

○ c. Boot Sector, BIOS, GUI, POST

○ d. POST, BIOS, Boot Sector, GUI

Question 46

A customer has brought a computer into your workplace for upgrading. You have interviewed the customer and discovered that she has done a full system backup, including the INI files. What other factors do you need to consider before performing the upgrade?

○ a. That the current OS can be upgraded and that RAM and hard disk space are adequate.

○ b. That the current OS can be upgraded and that the OS is not a pirated copy.

○ c. That the current OS can be upgraded and that the data files have been backed up.

○ d. That the current OS is registered and that the RAM is adequate.

Question 47

The standard policy of the company where you work is that all new Windows NT 4 computers must have an up-to-date emergency repair disk. From the command prompt, what command can you execute to create an emergency repair disk?

○ a. **FDISK**

○ b. **ERD**

○ c. **RDISK**

○ d. **FORMAT /ERD**

Question 48

A customer calls your tech support line and tells you that he has just purchased a new 20GB hard drive and installed a copy of Windows 98. When the customer looks at the drive in the Windows Explorer, the information reported is that it is only 2GB. You have confirmed that the drive is a 20GB hard drive based on the system CMOS/BIOS. What should you tell the customer to do in order to use the remaining 18GB?

- ○ a. Return the drive because it is defective.
- ○ b. Use the Disk Defragmenter to free up space.
- ○ c. Run FDISK and partition the remaining space.
- ○ d. Reformat the hard drive using NTFS.

Question 49

You have just installed the beta version of your company's Customer Management software on your Windows NT workstation. When you start the application, it conflicts with your word processing application. What can you do to temporarily fix this problem while you wait for the next version?

- ○ a. Tell your supervisor that everything works fine.
- ○ b. Run the beta program in protected memory space.
- ○ c. Run the beta program in shared memory space.
- ○ d. Run the beta program on a coworker's computer.

Question 50

A user on your NT network has forgotten her password. Where can you look to find the user's password so she can log on?

- ○ a. User Manager for Domains.
- ○ b. Password Manager for Networks.
- ○ c. Administrator Rights.
- ○ d. You must reset the user's password; it is not provided in clear text.

Question 51

A customer calls your help desk stating that he has just installed a new software DVD program in his Windows NT 4 computer. When he restarted the system, it went into the blue screen of death. What should you tell the customer to do to get the system to boot properly?

○ a. When NT starts, select Safe Mode with Network Support.

○ b. Have the customer physically remove the DVD drive.

○ c. Tell the customer to select the Last Known Good option.

○ d. Have the customer reformat the drive and reinstall Windows NT.

Question 52

A customer has called your help line stating that the taskbar on her Windows 2000 computer is at the top of the screen, and she doesn't know how it got there or how to put it back where it was. What is the easiest way to restore the taskbar to the bottom of the screen?

○ a. Restart the computer; it will automatically place the taskbar on the bottom.

○ b. Right-click the taskbar, select Properties, and check the box Place On Bottom.

○ c. Right-click the taskbar and select Auto Hide.

○ d. Left-click a blank area of the taskbar and hold the mouse button down, then drag the taskbar to the bottom of the screen and release the mouse button.

Question 53

You have just installed a new game on your Windows 98 computer that requires five CDs to install. After restarting your computer, you notice that the game runs slowly and that other applications are also running slowly. What are the most likely reasons?

○ a. Hard drive space and RAM

○ b. DirectX and video card

○ c. OpenGL and video card

○ d. Hard drive space and CD-ROM

Question 54

You are playing a game on your home network, and one of your new friends says the mouse isn't working. You go and inspect the mouse and discover the cursor is frozen. After restarting the system, the mouse cursor is still frozen. You take the mouse to another computer and it works fine. What is the most likely problem?

○ a. The mouse is broken.

○ b. The mouse has been disabled.

○ c. The mouse port is bad on the computer.

○ d. The mouse is not a Microsoft-compatible mouse.

Question 55

What can you type at the command prompt of a Windows NT 4 system to ensure that TCP/IP is working, even if you know the NIC is not functioning properly?

○ a. **Netstat -a**

○ b. **Nbtstat -s**

○ c. **Arp -rr**

○ d. **Ping 127.0.0.1**

Question 56

Which of the following error messages would you receive if the NTLDR.COM file became corrupted?

○ a. "Bad or Missing Command Interpreter"

○ b. "The Kernel File Is Missing from the Disk"

○ c. "Keyboard Missing, Press F1 to Continue"

○ d. "System Halted"

Question 57

You want to change the logical drive letter of your second hard drive on Windows 2000. Where would you look to find the tool that does this?

- ○ a. My Computer|Control Panel|Media
- ○ b. My Computer|Control Panel|Computer Management
- ○ c. My Computer|Control Panel|Logical Drives
- ○ d. My Computer|Control Panel|Administrative Tools|Computer Management

Question 58

You are printing from a Windows NT 4 workstation when the print job halts for no apparent reason. What is the first thing you should do to try to correct this problem?

- ○ a. Restart the spooler.
- ○ b. Resend the print job.
- ○ c. Restart the printer (turn power off then on).
- ○ d. Call the manufacturer's support line.

Question 59

You have installed a modem in your Windows 98 computer; however, when you try to connect to the Internet you get the error message: "No Dial Tone". You check your phone line and discover it is working properly. Where should you look next to find out if the device is functioning correctly?

- ○ a. System Info
- ○ b. SYSEDIT
- ○ c. WIN.INI
- ○ d. Device Manager

Question 60

Shared devices on Windows 98 use the NetBIOS protocol to identify themselves on the network. Where on Windows 98 can you view a list of resources others have shared out?

○ a. My Computer

○ b. Network Neighborhood

○ c. Windows Explorer

○ d. Taskbar

Question 61

What protocol ensures reliable delivery of packets over the Internet?

○ a. NetBIOS

○ b. UDP

○ c. ARP

○ d. TCP/IP

Question 62

A customer calls and tells you he is working from a Windows NT 4 workstation for the first time. He remembers looking at the boot drive of the computer with Windows Explorer and accidentally deleting a file. When the customer restarted the computer, it did not boot correctly. What file did he most probably delete?

○ a. BOOT.INI

○ b. SYSTEM.INI

○ c. WIN.INI

○ d. CPL.INI

Question 63

Which protocols allow the sharing of print devices in Windows 98?

○ a. ARP, UDP, NetBIOS

○ b. NetBEUI, IPX/SPX, TCP/IP

○ c. NetBIOS, TCP/IP, ARP

○ d. TCP/IP, IPX/SPX, SMTP

Question 64

Using only Windows 98, what type of network can you set up?

○ a. Client/server

○ b. IEEE 2001.1

○ c. Peer-to-peer

○ d. ATM

Question 65

You are printing from a Windows 98 computer when you receive an "Out of Memory" error message. After verifying that you have plenty of hard drive space, what should you do next?

○ a. Restart the spooler.

○ b. Install more RAM.

○ c. Reinstall the print driver.

○ d. Uninstall the printer and reinstall the driver on another logical drive.

Question 66

What mode of operation is available in Windows 98 to allow you to boot to the GUI if you improperly configure a display driver?

○ a. Minimal

○ b. Typical

○ c. Normal

○ d. Safe

Question 67

Of the following, which is an example of a UNC?

○ a. \\Computer name\Resource name

○ b. http://Domain name/Web page name

○ c. \\Domain name\Computer name\Resource name

○ d. https://Secure Domain name/Web page name

Question 68

Of the following, which is an example of a FQDN?

○ a. **www.serverx.xdomain.net**

○ b. **xdomain.net**

○ c. **xdomain.com**

○ d. **http://207.231.225.147**

Question 69

Of the following, which is an incorrect entry in the Web browser's address box?

○ a. **ftp://examcram.com**

○ b. **http://examcram.com**

○ c. **http://www.examcram.com**

○ d. **dns://examcram.com**

Question 70

You have been assigned by the systems administrator to deploy a new Windows 2000 installation across a new office network. What tool is available with Windows 2000 that will help you track information about the computers and users for whom you perform the installation?

- ○ a. RIS
- ○ b. FDISK
- ○ c. ERD
- ○ d. Active Directory

A+ OS Technologies
Answer Key #2

1. a	19. d	37. c	55. d
2. b	20. b	38. d	56. b
3. c	21. b	39. c	57. d
4. d	22. a	40. a	58. a
5. b	23. b	41. b	59. d
6. a	24. d	42. c	60. b
7. d	25. b	43. c	61. d
8. b	26. a	44. a	62. a
9. b	27. a	45. d	63. b
10. c	28. d	46. a	64. c
11. a	29. b	47. c	65. b
12. c	30. d	48. c	66. d
13. b	31. d	49. b	67. a
14. d	32. a	50. d	68. a
15. c	33. a	51. c	69. d
16. c	34. c	52. d	70. d
17. c	35. a	53. a	
18. a	36. b	54. b	

Question 1

The correct answer is a. When the computer first boots, it must load the basic input/output system (BIOS), then the Real Mode MS-DOS drivers are loaded to give access to devices that have been added to the physical computer, then Windows can begin to take over from DOS and load its Protected Mode. Another way to think of this is: first power, then DOS, then Windows. Answer b is incorrect because BIOS is required to be loaded before the Real Mode drivers. Answer c is incorrect because Real Mode VxD Loader cannot load without the Real Mode DOS drivers. Answer d is incorrect for the same reason c is incorrect: The VxD loading cannot occur without the MS-DOS drivers loading.

For more information on this topic, see *A+ Exam Cram, 2nd Edition*, Chapter 12, the section "Start Sequence".

Question 2

The correct answer is b. The IO.SYS and MSDOS.SYS files load nearly simultaneously and use functions from one another to load the CONFIG.SYS file. CONFIG.SYS then calls the COMMAND.COM file into memory so that it can interpret the internal commands issued in the AUTOEXEC.BAT file, such as "Path". Answer a is incorrect because the Command Interpreter (COMMAND.COM) cannot function without the help of IO.SYS and MS-DOS.SYS. Answer c is incorrect because the CONFIG.SYS file requires the IO.SYS and MS-DOS.SYS files to be loaded first. Answer d is incorrect because AUTOEXEC.BAT is dependent on the Command Interpreter to be loaded first.

For more information on this topic, see *A+ Exam Cram, 2nd Edition*, Chapter 12, the section "Starting Windows 9x".

Question 3

The correct answer is c. The Exclude option of EMM386 is denoted with an "X" for exclude. You could also think of this as "X" marking out an area. Answer a is incorrect because the / is not required in EMM386 and the NoEMS is not a valid switch. There is also a subtle hint in the case of the letters to tell you that this answer is incorrect: DOS does not distinguish between upper- and lowercase. Answer b is incorrect because NOEMS is not a valid switch. Answer d is incorrect because the "E" is not used for excluding.

For more information on this topic, see *A+ Exam Cram, 2nd Edition*, Chapter 11, the section "HIMEM.SYS and EMM386.EXE".

Question 4

The correct answer is d. The relatively small size of floppy drives uses FAT-12 (the 12 stands for 12-bit binary values), which accommodates relatively small cluster-size disks. To date there has been no call to change to a FAT-16 or FAT-32 for standard floppy disks. Answer a is incorrect because FAT-32 is used for hard drives. Answer b is incorrect because FAT-16 is the current default FAT used on hard drives, sometimes called V-FAT. Answer c is incorrect because there is no such thing used on Microsoft operating systems.

For more information on this topic, see *A+ Exam Cram, 2nd Edition*, Chapter 13, the section "NT File System (NTFS)".

Question 5

The correct answer is b. The primary partition is where the system will boot from initially; the system BIOS has already reserved the label of C: for this drive, and therefore the primary partition must always be labeled C:. Answer a is incorrect because the attribute of "active" can be assigned to any drive letter. Answer c is incorrect because there are only 24 extended partitions available. Answer d is incorrect because FDISK will not partition floppy disks.

For more information on this topic, see *A+ Exam Cram, 2nd Edition*, Chapter 6, the section "Fixed Disks/Hard Drives".

Question 6

The correct answer is a. MSDOS.SYS, IO.SYS and COMMAND.COM are the files required to boot from floppy. Answer b is incorrect because without IO.SYS the command interpreter will not get loaded. Answers c and d are incorrect because without MSDOS.SYS the command interpreter will not get loaded.

For more information on this topic, see *A+ Exam Cram, 2nd Edition*, Chapter 11, the section "The Bootable Disk".

Question 7

The correct answer is d. When using DOS (FAT-16) file names there can be no special characters in the file name. Answer a is incorrect because the % sign is a special character. Answer b is incorrect because the + sign is a special character. Answer c is incorrect because the $ sign is a special character.

For more information on this topic, see *A+ Exam Cram, 2nd Edition*, Chapter 10, the section "File Names".

Question 8

The correct answer is b. This is the only choice that includes three of the six primary Windows 9x files, which are: USER.EXE, USER32.EXE, GDI.EXE, GDI32.EXE, KRNL386.EXE, and KRNL38632.EXE. Answer a is incorrect because these are two configuration files and a utility. Answer c is incorrect because these files are mainly DOS files. Answer d is incorrect because NTLDR.EXE is a Windows NT file, not a Windows 9x file.

For more information on this topic, see *A+ Exam Cram, 2nd Edition*, Chapter 12, the section "Final Steps to Loading Windows 9x".

Question 9

The correct answer is b. SYSEDIT is a utility included in Windows 9x that opens all the files that normally require editing when a device is added to the system. Answers a, c, and d are incorrect because normally you don't need to edit CONTROL.INI or PROGMAN.INI.

For more information on this topic, see *A+ Exam Cram, 2nd Edition*, Chapter 11, the section "Initialization (INI) Files".

Question 10

The correct answer is c. The SPART.PAR and the 386SPART.PAR files are both permanent swap files. Answer a is incorrect because WIN386.SWP is the name of a temporary swap file. Answer b is incorrect because you would not be able to determine if the file is corrupt in Windows Explorer. Answer d is incorrect because SPART.PAR is the name of the permanent swap file.

For more information on this topic, see *A+ Exam Cram, 2nd Edition*, Chapter 11, the section "Memory".

Question 11

The correct answer is a. To ease administration efforts, DHCP is employed on a network. This allows the computer to configure the IP settings automatically. The DHCP process starts when the computer is first turned on. The NIC sends a signal to the DCHP server letting the server know it is ready to obtain an address and related information. Answer b is incorrect because a DNS server is used to resolve host names to IP addresses. Answer c is incorrect because WINS is used to resolve NetBIOS names. Answer d is incorrect because it is used for sending email.

For more information on this topic, see *A+ Exam Cram, 2nd Edition*, Chapter 13, the section "Windows 2000 Diagnostics and Troubleshooting".

Question 12

The correct answer is c. Windows 9x has two basic types of access available for sharing resources: share-level and user-level. In the case of share-level access, the user is prompted to enter a password to gain access to the resource. In the case of user-level, access to the resource is determined by your accounts' permissions. Answer a is incorrect because not everyone will be able to enter the shared resources. Answer b is incorrect because anyone with the correct password on the network will be able to access the resource, not just administrators. Answer d is incorrect because this is an example of user-level security.

For more information on this topic, see *A+ Exam Cram, 2nd Edition*, Chapter 8, the section "Networking Overview".

Question 13

The correct answer is b. The 8.3 character convention does not allow for the use of spaces in the name. Also, the Windows 9x operating system defaults to adding a ~ (tilde) plus the number of times that particular 8.3 file name has been used. For example, the first occurrence will be xxxxxx~1.xxx, the second will be xxxxxx~2.xxx, and so forth. The easiest way to figure out the answer to this type of question is to simply count every character, excluding special characters, keeping in mind that a ~ and a number will take up the last 2 characters. The file extension will remain the same. Answer a is incorrect because there are more characters in the initial name than appear in the answer. Answer c is incorrect because spaces are not allowed in the 8.3 format. Answer d is incorrect because the ~ is in the wrong place.

For more information on this topic, see *A+ Exam Cram, 2nd Edition*, Chapter 12, the section "The Installable File System (IFS) Managers".

Question 14

The correct answer is d. The addition of the Registry in Windows 9x helps maintain a stable system even when other devices are added or removed. The Registry is composed of the SYSTEM.DAT and the USER.DAT files. Answer a is incorrect because the answer lists DOS files. Answer b is incorrect because REGEDIT is a program used to edit the Registry, and REG.SYS is a made-up file name. Answer c is incorrect because USER.EXE and SYSTEM.INI have the correct file names but not the correct extensions.

For more information on this topic, see *A+ Exam Cram, 2nd Edition*, Chapter 12, the section "The Registry".

Question 15

The correct answer is c. The long file names (LFNs) have taken up the maximum space on the operating system. In Windows 9x, the maximum number of directory entries in the root FAT table is 512. Answer a is incorrect because the scenario told you that you verified the amount of available space. Answer b is incorrect because this has nothing to do with the creation of folders. Answer d is incorrect because you can create directories off the root directory.

For more information on this topic, see *A+ Exam Cram, 2nd Edition*, Chapter 10, the section "File Systems".

Question 16

The correct answer is c. To boot to a previous version of an operating system, press the F4 key while Windows first boots up. Answer a is incorrect because Ctrl+Alt+Del will bring up the Task Manager or restart the system. Answer b is incorrect because F8 gives you multiple choices. Answer d is incorrect because F5 will take you to Safe Mode.

For more information on this topic, see *A+ Exam Cram, 2nd Edition*, Chapter 12, the section "Startup Menu (F8) and Safe Mode".

Question 17

The correct answer is c. COMMAND.COM is the command interpreter for MS-DOS. Answer a is incorrect because IO.SYS is a file that must be loaded prior to COMMAND.COM. Answer b is incorrect because MSDOS.SYS is a file that must be loaded prior to COMMAND.COM. Answer d is incorrect because WIN.COM is the file that starts Windows—you would be well past getting this error message if the system couldn't load WIN.COM.

For more information on this topic, see *A+ Exam Cram, 2nd Edition*, Chapter 10, the section "The Command Interpreter".

Question 18

The correct answer is a. By right-clicking Network Neighborhood, you can access the Network Properties; then if you click the Access Control tab, you will see the options for the type of security you want to use. Answer b is incorrect because the Internet Explorer settings are for the Internet. Answer c is incorrect because the Users And Groups icon in the Control Panel is for creating and managing user accounts. Answer d is incorrect because User Level Security is not an option when you right-click the Start button.

For more information on this topic, see *A+ Exam Cram, 2nd Edition*, Chapter 14, the section "Connectivity Problems".

Question 19

The correct answer is d. The NT File System (NTFS) is not supported in Windows 9x. Answer a is incorrect because all Windows-based systems will read floppy disks, which use FAT-12. Answer b is incorrect because FAT-32 is the preferred file system of Windows 9x. Answer c is incorrect because all Windows-based systems will read drives formatted with FAT-16.

For more information on this topic, see *A+ Exam Cram, 2nd Edition*, Chapter 13, the section "NT File System (NTFS)".

Question 20

The correct answer is b. Windows NT 4 cannot read FAT-32 hard drives by default. Answer a is incorrect because all Windows-based systems can read floppy disks, which are formatted with FAT-12. Answer c is incorrect because all Windows-based systems can read drives formatted with FAT-16. Answer d is incorrect because NTFS is the preferred format for Windows NT.

For more information on this topic, see *A+ Exam Cram, 2nd Edition*, Chapter 13, the section "NT Workstation and NT Server".

Question 21

The correct answer is b. Windows 2000 supports the FAT-32 file system. Answer a is incorrect because all Windows-based systems can read floppy disks, which are formatted with FAT-12. Answer c is incorrect because all Windows-based systems can read hard disks formatted with FAT-16. Answer d is incorrect because NTFS is the preferred format for all current versions of Windows NT.

For more information on this topic, see *A+ Exam Cram, 2ⁿᵈ Edition*, Chapter 13, the section "NT File System (NTFS)".

Question 22

The correct answer is a. The 16-bit executable setup file is **WINNT.EXE**. Answer b is incorrect because **WINNT32.EXE** is not for DOS-based installations. Answer c is incorrect because **WIN2K.EXE** is not an installation file. Answer d is incorrect because **SETUP.EXE** is the command for setting up Windows 9x.

For more information on this topic, see *A+ Exam Cram, 2ⁿᵈ Edition*, Chapter 13, the section "Troubleshooting Tools".

Question 23

The correct answer is b. Windows 98 is a 32-bit operating system and so you issue the 32-bit command **WINNT32.EXE**. Answer a is incorrect because **WINNT.EXE** is for DOS-based installations. Answer c is incorrect because **WIN2K.EXE** is not an installation file. Answer d is incorrect because **SETUP.EXE** is the command for setting up Microsoft Windows 9x.

For more information on this topic, see *A+ Exam Cram, 2ⁿᵈ Edition*, Chapter 12, the section "Installing Windows 95, 98, and ME".

Question 24

The correct answer is d. **SETUP.EXE** is the command that starts the installation process of Windows 98. Answer a is incorrect because **WIN98.EXE** is not an installation file. Answer b is incorrect because **WIN.EXE** is the command used to start Windows after it is installed. Answer c is incorrect because **WINME.EXE** is not an installation file.

For more information on this topic, see *A+ Exam Cram, 2ⁿᵈ Edition*, Chapter 12, the section "Installing Windows 95, 98, and ME".

Question 25

The correct answer is b. A red X will appear next to the device in the Device Manager for items that have been disabled. Answer a is incorrect because that is the symbol for a device that is functioning but has conflicts. Answers c and d are incorrect because there are no such symbols in Windows 9x Device Manager.

For more information on this topic, see *A+ Exam Cram, 2nd Edition*, Chapter 13, the section "Windows 2000 Diagnostics and Troubleshooting".

Question 26

The correct answer is a. *Thunking* is the term given to calling 16-bit programs into 32-bit programs. Answer b is incorrect because thrashing is a made-up answer. Answer c is incorrect because corruption is when a file becomes unreadable. Answer d is incorrect because truncating is the process of removing invalid or unusable characters from a string.

For more information on this topic, see *A+ Exam Cram, 2nd Edition*, Chapter 12, the section "Windows 9x vs. Windows 3.x".

Question 27

The correct answer is a. Windows has programs running in the background that attempt to recover from unstable situations; you need to give them time to work. Then, if the programs don't terminate the hung application, you should open the Task Manager and help out with the process by ending the task that is not responding. Once the task that is not responding has closed, save your work from the running application and reboot your system. Answer b is incorrect because hitting the reset button before saving your work will not meet the requirements of the question. Answer c is incorrect because ending the program that is running will not meet the requirements of the question. Answer d is incorrect because once a shutdown is started, the subsystems that attempt to recover from an error are halted.

For more information on this topic, see *A+ Exam Cram, 2nd Edition*, Chapter 13, the section "Troubleshooting Tools".

Question 28

The correct answer is d. The AUTOEXEC.BAT file is where you set up the DOS prompt by default. **Prompt=PG** will set the command prompt to *drive + parent directory* + greater-than sign (**C:\>** if in the root directory). Answer a is incorrect because CONFIG.SYS is where device drivers are set up in DOS. Answer b is incorrect because WIN.INI is for settings in Windows. Answer c is incorrect because SYSTEM.INI is where the Windows system is configured.

For more information on this topic, see *A+ Exam Cram, 2nd Edition*, Chapter 10, the section "Batch Files".

Question 29

The correct answer is b. Windows 95 shares memory space by default with all Windows-based applications. Answer a is incorrect because Windows runs 32-bit applications in their own memory space by default. Answer c is incorrect because not all applications are Windows-based. Answer d is incorrect because Internet-aware programs could be 16- or 32-bit, but being Internet aware does not necessarily imply that the application is Windows-based.

For more information on this topic, see *A+ Exam Cram, 2nd Edition*, Chapter 11, the section "Windows".

Question 30

The correct answer is d. Disabling the Protected Mode disk drivers will force Windows to use the Real Mode drivers. Answer a is incorrect because disabling file sharing will only disable shared resources. Answer b is incorrect because it implies that the drive is supported; otherwise it couldn't do write-behind caching. Answer c is incorrect for the same reason answer b; it implies that the disk is compatible.

For more information on this topic, see *A+ Exam Cram, 2nd Edition*, Chapter 12, the section "Windows 9x vs. Windows 3.x".

Question 31

The correct answer is d. In Windows 98, all 32-bit applications by default run in their own memory space. Answer a is incorrect because 16- and 32-bit applications run in separate memory. Answer b is incorrect because 32-bit applications run in their own memory space. Answer c is incorrect because 16- and 32-bit applications do not share the same memory space.

For more information on this topic, see *A+ Exam Cram, 2nd Edition*, Chapter 14, the section "Startup Problems".

Question 32

The correct answer is a. While installing a Windows 9x computer on a network, you are asked for several things, but in order for the computer to be recognized on the network it must have a Username, a Computer Name, and a Workgroup or Domain Name. Answer b is incorrect because DNS is not required for the network. Answer c is incorrect because IIS is not required unless it's going to be a Web server. Answer d is incorrect because you could use a static IP address, thus it is not "required".

For more information on this topic, see *A+ Exam Cram, 2nd Edition*, Chapter 12, the section "Installing Windows 95, 98, and ME".

Question 33

The correct answer is a. Network Neighborhood is a standalone icon on the desktop by default if you install networking components. Answer b is incorrect because Dial-Up Networking is in the Control Panel. Answer c is incorrect because Modems is in the Control Panel. Answer d is incorrect because Add/Remove Programs is also in the Control Panel.

For more information on this topic, see *A+ Exam Cram, 2nd Edition*, Chapter 14, the section "Diagnostics Tools".

Question 34

The correct answer is c. When a device is detected, it is installed by default, even if it doesn't work properly. In the case where a device driver is not found or the device has conflicts with another device on the system, a yellow circle with a black exclamation point is shown next to the device in the Device Manager. Answer a is incorrect, but tricky because this may be the reason the symbol is there. Answer b is incorrect because there is no symbol in the Device Manager that means "restart." Answer d is incorrect because there is no symbol in Device Manager that means a device is incompatible.

For more information on this topic, see *A+ Exam Cram, 2nd Edition*, Chapter 13, the section "Windows 2000 Diagnostics and Troubleshooting".

Question 35

The correct answer is a. By default the system files, which include INIs, DLLs and INFs, are hidden from the end user in Windows Explorer view. Answers b, c, and d are incorrect because you can see VXDs, BAT files, and EXEs.

For more information on this topic, see *A+ Exam Cram, 2nd Edition*, Chapter 12, the section "Windows 98".

Question 36

The correct answer is b. ScanDisk can be used to detect and repair common problems with floppy and hard disk drives. Answer a is incorrect because ScanDisk is not able to fix problems on a CD-RW or CD-R. Answer c is incorrect because ScanDisk is not able to fix Zip disk problems. Answer d is incorrect for the same reason answer a is incorrect; ScanDisk is not for fixing problems with CD-RWs.

For more information on this topic, see *A+ Exam Cram, 2nd Edition*, Chapter 10, the section "File Management".

Question 37

The correct answer is c. The **DIR** or "directory" command is included as part of the internal workings of MSDOS.SYS, IO.SYS, and COMMAND.COM. Any command that is called from those files is termed an "internal" command. Answer a is incorrect because **EDIT** is its own application that requires it be called into the command interpreter. Answer b is incorrect because **XCOPY** is its own application that requires it to be called into the command interpreter as well. Answer d is incorrect because **DELTREE** is also its own application. An easier way to think about this might be as follows: If it has an *executable* command in DOS, then it's *external*.

For more information on this topic, see *A+ Exam Cram, 2nd Edition*, Chapter 10, the section "DOS Commands".

Question 38

The correct answer is d. **XCOPY** has its own application, meaning there is an XCOPY.EXE file, and so it is not incorporated into the command interpreter. This makes it an "external" command. Answers a, b, and c are incorrect because with the basic files required to boot, you can execute **DIR, MD,** and **SET**.

For more information on this topic, see *A+ Exam Cram, 2nd Edition*, Chapter 10, the section "DOS Commands".

Question 39

The correct answer is c. COMMAND.COM is the command interpreter for DOS-based applications. Answer a is incorrect because IO.SYS establishes the Input-Output basic system. Answer b is incorrect because MSDOS.SYS combined with IO.SYS initializes the system. Answer d is incorrect because EDIT.EXE is used for editing.

For more information on this topic, see *A+ Exam Cram, 2nd Edition*, Chapter 10, the section "DOS Commands".

Question 40

The correct answer is a. When you install Windows NT, you are creating the administrator account by default. This is done because only the administrator has full rights to configure the system, which is part of the installation process. Answer b is incorrect because the system would not be able to configure itself if the installer did not have administrative rights and privileges. Answer c is incorrect for the same reason answer b is incorrect: Administrative rights and privileges are required to install and configure the entire installation. Answer d is incorrect for the same reasons answers b and c are incorrect.

For more information on this topic, see *A+ Exam Cram, 2nd Edition*, Chapter 13, the section "User Accounts".

Question 41

The correct answer is b. After opening My Computer, you can get the properties of a hard drive by right-clicking it; from there you can choose the Tools tab and then click Defragment Now. Answer a is incorrect because the System icon is not in My Computer (it is in Control Panel). Answer c is incorrect because Add New Hardware is also in Control Panel, not to mention that it is not used for disk defragmenting. Answer d is incorrect because on Windows 2000, the Disk Defragmenter is started using the My Computer icon or Start|Programs|Accessories|System Tools|Disk Defragmenter.

For more information on this topic, see *A+ Exam Cram, 2nd Edition*, Chapter 13, the section "Troubleshooting Tools".

Question 42

The correct answer is c. After opening My Computer, you can right-click on the hard drive to access its Properties, then select the Tools tab and run the Disk Defragmenter. Answer a is incorrect because there is no Disk Defragmenter icon in My Computer. Answer b is incorrect because there is no Tools icon in My Computer. Answer d is incorrect because there is no Advanced option from the Properties menu of a hard drive when accessed through My Computer.

For more information on this topic, see *A+ Exam Cram, 2nd Edition*, Chapter 12, the section "Windows 9x vs. Windows 3.x".

Question 43

The correct answer is c. When you open the My Computer icon from the desktop, several things are displayed, including the hard drives. To access the properties of a hard drive, you right-click the hard drive you want and click Properties. Answer a is incorrect because double-clicking will open a view of the hard drive. Answer b is incorrect because there is no Properties icon. Answer d is also incorrect because there is no Properties icon.

For more information on this topic, see *A+ Exam Cram, 2nd Edition*, Chapter 12, the section "Windows 9x vs. Windows 3.x".

Question 44

The correct answer is a. The command interpreter gets modified/moved because in order for the bootstrap to load the new NT installation, the NT boot loader must be read first so that it can call the multiboot file. Answer b is incorrect because no changes are made to the IO.SYS file. Answer c is incorrect because no changes are made to the MSDOS.SYS file. Answer d is incorrect because this is not an NT file.

For more information on this topic, see *A+ Exam Cram, 2nd Edition*, Chapter 13, the section "NT Disk Administration".

Question 45

The correct answer is d. The Power On Self Test (POST) occurs before the basic input/output system (BIOS) is loaded. Once BIOS is established, the Boot Sector can be read, and then the graphical user interface (GUI) can load. Answer a is incorrect because the BIOS cannot load before the POST has been completed. Answer b is incorrect because the GUI can't load without the system being started. Answer c is incorrect because the Boot Sector can't be read before the system starts.

For more information on this topic, see *A+ Exam Cram, 2nd Edition*, Chapter 11, the section "Booting and System Files".

Question 46

The correct answer is a. Prior to performing an upgrade, it is recommended that you back up all data from the hard drive. The INI files contain the changes to the program the user has made, such as color schemes or the buttons available on toolbars. Beyond making sure you can restore the user's previous settings, you must check to be sure that the current operating system can be upgraded, including that there is sufficient RAM and Hard Disk space. Answers b, c, and d are incorrect because they do not take into account the system requirements.

For more information on this topic, see *A+ Exam Cram, 2nd Edition*, Chapter 11, the section "Initialization (INI) Files".

Question 47

The correct answer is c. The **RDISK** command is used to create an emergency repair disk (ERD). This is not to say that it will run in the DOS window; in fact, it will bring up a GUI application. Answer a is incorrect because **FDISK** is for partitioning disks. Answer b is incorrect because there is no such command. Answer d is incorrect because **/ERD** is not a supported option of **FORMAT**.

For more information on this topic, see *A+ Exam Cram, 2nd Edition*, Chapter 13, the section "NT Workstation and NT Server".

Question 48

The correct answer is c. **FDISK** is the utility used with Windows 98 operating systems to create partitions. In this case, the scenario is that the customer can only see one 2GB partition. Beyond running **FDISK** in order for the new partition to store information, the new partition will need to be formatted. In this case, the customer probably did not enable Large Block Architecture (LBA) and has a partition size limit of 2GB. Answer a is incorrect because you were able to verify the drive through the BIOS; it's way too early in the troubleshooting process to pronounce it defective. Answer b is incorrect because the total drive space is the issue, not available drive space. Answer d is incorrect because although NTFS can be used on large partitions, it is not a way to partition the drive in the first place. Also, NTFS is not a supported file system on Windows 98.

For more information on this topic, see *A+ Exam Cram, 2nd Edition*, Chapter10, the section "Logical Formatting and Partitions: **FDISK**".

Question 49

The correct answer is b. Windows NT allows you to run programs in protected memory space so that if one crashes, it is the only application that is affected. Answer a is incorrect because there is a problem. Answer c is incorrect because shared memory space is what is most likely causing the problem. Answer d is incorrect because although it might solve the problem for you, it doesn't really solve the problem.

For more information on this topic, see *A+ Exam Cram, 2nd Edition*, Chapter 11, the section "Windows".

Question 50

The correct answer is d. User passwords are protected by masking characters such as ****** , which is done for security. In NT, the administrator doesn't need to know a user's password; the administrator can access a machine and its files simply by logging on as the administrator from the workstation if he or she needs access. Answer a is incorrect because this will only show the masked password. Answer b is incorrect because there is no Password Manager for Networks application on NT. Answer c is incorrect because there is no Administrator Rights application on NT.

For more information on this topic, see *A+ Exam Cram, 2nd Edition*, Chapter 13, the section "User Accounts".

Question 51

The correct answer is c. The Last Known Good option loads the driver set of the last known good boot up. This question is typical of the harder questions on the certification test; DVD devices are not supported on NT 4 and might lead you to believe that the DVD drive is the problem. However, DVD drives can be installed on NT 4 default installations, and they will be read and used as a CD drive. In this case, however, the question specifically states that software has been added. Answer a is incorrect because although the system will boot, Safe Mode has very limited options—it's not a normal boot. Answer b is incorrect because the DVD drive will be read as a normal CD. Answer d is incorrect because it requires more effort than selecting Last Known Good.

For more information on this topic, see *A+ Exam Cram, 2nd Edition*, Chapter 14, the section "Startup Problems".

Question 52

The correct answer is d. By left-clicking and holding down the mouse button, you can drag the taskbar where you want it. When you release the mouse button, the taskbar will stay in the position you dragged it to until you move it again. Answer a is incorrect because when the taskbar is moved, its position is remembered, so when the system restarts, it is where you left it last. Answer b is incorrect because there is no option in the Properties of the taskbar labeled Place On Bottom. Answer c is incorrect because this will not move the taskbar.

For more information on this topic, see *A+ Exam Cram, 2nd Edition*, Chapter 13, the section "Troubleshooting Tools".

Question 53

The correct answer is a. The question implies that the installation took a bit of hard drive space. Most large applications also require large amounts of RAM. Windows 98 systems run slower when the disk drive is nearly full. Answer b is incorrect because prior to the new game installation run better, most likely the video card and corresponding display drivers are fine. Answer c is incorrect for the same reason answer b is incorrect. Answer d is incorrect because the other applications most likely run from the hard drive.

For more information on this topic, see *A+ Exam Cram, 2ⁿᵈ Edition*, Chapter 12, the section "Windows 95, 98, and ME".

Question 54

The correct answer is b. From the options given, the most likely cause is that the mouse has been disabled. If the mouse cursor appears on startup of Windows, the mouse was detected. When you are unable to move the mouse cursor and you have eliminated faulty hardware as the cause, check in the Device Manager to see if there are conflicts or if a device has been disabled. Answer a is incorrect because you verified that the mouse worked on another computer. Answer c is incorrect because the cursor appears when you start the computer. When a mouse is installed properly, it will display a cursor. Answer d is incorrect because the question implies that the mouse worked before.

For more information on this topic, see *A+ Exam Cram, 2ⁿᵈ Edition*, Chapter 13, the section "Windows 2000 Diagnostics and Troubleshooting".

Question 55

The correct answer is d. To check if TCP/IP is correctly installed, you can **ping** your reserved IP address for the local machine: 127.0.0.1. Doing this does not indicate anything other than that TCP/IP is installed. Answer a is incorrect because **Netstat** displays the network status. Answer b is incorrect because **Nbtstat** shows information about the NetBIOS sessions. Answer c is incorrect because the Address Resolution Protocol (ARP) does not have a diagnostic switch.

For more information on this topic, see *A+ Exam Cram, 2ⁿᵈ Edition*, Chapter 14, the section "Connectivity Problems".

Question 56

The correct answer is b. When NTLDR is missing or corrupt, the error message you see on the screen is "The Kernel File Is Missing from the Disk" Answer a is incorrect because this is the error message for a missing or corrupted COMMAND.COM file. Answer c is incorrect because this is an error message from the BIOS. Answer d is incorrect because this is an error from an incomplete POST or an error detected from the BIOS.

For more information on this topic, see *A+ Exam Cram, 2nd Edition*, Chapter 13, the section "Starting Windows NT".

Question 57

The correct answer is d. To access the Disk Manager from the Control Panel on Windows 2000, double-click Administrative Tools and then the Computer Management icon. Answer a is incorrect because Media is where you configure things like your sound card. Answer b is incorrect because you must get into Administrative Tools from the Control Panel before you can access Computer Management. Answer c is incorrect because there is no Logical Drives icon in the Control Panel.

For more information on this topic, see *A+ Exam Cram, 2nd Edition*, Chapter 13, the section "NT Disk Administration".

Question 58

The correct answer is a. When a print job hangs in NT 4, barring physical problems, the culprit is usually the spooler service or a corrupted device driver. In this case, you don't have "device driver" as one of the options. Answer b is incorrect because all that resending the job will do is place the job in the print queue. Answer c is incorrect because turning the printer off and on will not restart the spooler service and will cause whatever is in printer memory to be lost—it might make the problem worse. Answer d is incorrect because you have not taken all the steps available to you yet; it's too early in the troubleshooting process to be calling the manufacturer.

For more information on this topic, see *A+ Exam Cram, 2nd Edition*, Chapter 14, the section "Services Icon".

Question 59

The correct answer is d. The Device Manager shows the state of the devices attached to your system. Regardless of the error message, if you have eliminated physical reasons for a device failure, the next place to look is in the Device Manager to be sure that the device is recognized and functioning properly. Answer a is incorrect because System Info will not tell you if the device is functioning properly, only what resources it is using. Answer b is incorrect because the SYSEDIT program is for editing configuration files. Answer c is incorrect because WIN.INI is the configuration for your Windows startup.

For more information on this topic, see *A+ Exam Cram, 2nd Edition*, Chapter 13, the section "Windows 2000 Diagnostics and Troubleshooting".

Question 60

The correct answer is b. The Network Neighborhood icon gives you a graphical look at other computers and resources on the network. Answer a is incorrect because the My Computer icon by default only shows the resources of your computer. Answer c is incorrect because from Windows Explorer you would have to choose Network Neighborhood to get a view of other computers and resources. Answer d is incorrect because the taskbar shows the tasks launched.

For more information on this topic, see *A+ Exam Cram, 2nd Edition*, Chapter 14, the section "Connectivity Problems".

Question 61

The correct answer is d. One of the reasons TCP/IP has become the default protocol of the Internet is its ability to ensure reliable delivery of packets. Answer a is incorrect because NetBIOS is a nonroutable protocol. Answer b is incorrect because UDP doesn't check to be sure the information is completely received. Answer c is incorrect because ARP is used as an announcement that the system is ready to receive TCP/IP information from a DHCP server.

For more information on this topic, see *A+ Exam Cram, 2nd Edition*, Chapter 8, the section "Bridges and Routers".

Question 62

The correct answer is a. The BOOT.INI file contains the information about in which partitions and drives the operating system is located. Without this file, the system will not know where to start from. Answer b is incorrect because SYSTEM.INI is a file that loads after boot up. Answer c is incorrect for the same reason answer b is incorrect; WIN.INI loads after boot up. Answer d is incorrect for the same reason answers b and c are incorrect; the system would have to have booted for CPL.INI to load.

For more information on this topic, see *A+ Exam Cram, 2nd Edition*, Chapter 13, the section "NT Error Messages".

Question 63

The correct answer is b. NetBEUI, IPX/SPX, and TCP/IP all allow you to share resources. Answer a is incorrect because ARP is for announcing the computer on the network to get TCP/IP information. Answer c is incorrect for the same reason answer a is incorrect; ARP is for address resolution, not sharing. Answer d is incorrect because Simple Mail Transfer Protocol (SMTP) is for email, not sharing devices.

For more information on this topic, see *A+ Exam Cram, 2nd Edition*, Chapter 13, the section "Windows 2000 Diagnostics and Troubleshooting".

Question 64

The correct answer is c. A network consisting of only Windows 98 computers does not have a dedicated server for providing centralized management. In this type of network, each computer is both a client and the server; this is why the term is *peer-to-peer*. Answer a is incorrect because using only Windows 98, you have no centralized management of resources or accounts. Answer b is incorrect because IEEE 2001.1 is a made-up specification. Answer d is incorrect because ATM is not a network type.

For more information on this topic, see *A+ Exam Cram, 2nd Edition*, Chapter 8, the section "Networking Overview".

Question 65

The correct answer is b. The question does not say the printer hangs, and you have enough hard drive space; therefore, the only other memory option available in this question is RAM. Answer a is incorrect because the question doesn't say the print job hung or failed. Answer c is incorrect because the print job doesn't fail and the printer didn't stall. Answer d is incorrect for the same reason answer c is incorrect.

For more information on this topic, see *A+ Exam Cram, 2nd Edition*, Chapter 14, the section "Hardware Problems".

Question 66

The correct answer is d. Safe Mode allows you to recover from improperly configured device drivers so that you can make changes. Answer a is incorrect because
Minimal is an installation option not an operation mode. Answer b is incorrect
because Typical is an installation option not an operation mode. Answer c is incorrect because the problem is that the computer is not booting into normal mode.

For more information on this topic, see *A+ Exam Cram, 2ⁿᵈ Edition*, Chapter 14,
the section "Startup Problems".

Question 67

The correct answer is a. The Universal Naming Convention (UNC) consists of the
computer name, where the resource is located, and the share name of the resource
in a Microsoft network. Answer b is incorrect because it is an example of a Uniform
Resource Locator (URL). Answer c is incorrect because the domain name is not
part of the UNC. Answer d is incorrect because it is also an example of a URL.

For more information on this topic, see *A+ Exam Cram, 2ⁿᵈ Edition*, Chapter 8,
the section "Networking Overview".

Question 68

The correct answer is a. A Fully Qualified Domain Name (FQDN) consists of all
the identifiers. In this case, the domain is a World Wide Web domain, the computer name is **serverx**, the name of the domain is **xdomain**, and it is a network.
Answer b is incorrect because this could be any type of domain—it could be a
local area domain or an Internet domain; it hasn't been qualified. Answer c is
incorrect for the same reason answer b is incorrect. Answer d is incorrect because
it's not a domain name at all—it's an IP address to a domain.

For more information on this topic, see *A+ Exam Cram, 2ⁿᵈ Edition*, Chapter 8,
the section "Networking Overview".

Question 69

The correct answer is d. DNS is a service, not a supported protocol. Answers a, b, and
c are incorrect because they reference valid protocol types: File Transfer Protocol
(FTP) and Hypertext Transport Protocol (HTTP).

For more information on this topic, see *A+ Exam Cram, 2ⁿᵈ Edition*, Chapter 8,
the section "Networking Overview".

Question 70

The correct answer is d. Active Directory acts as a catalog of all systems resources. Answer a is incorrect because Remote Installation Service (RIS) is for performing the installation only. Answer b is incorrect because FDISK is for partitioning drives. Answer c is incorrect because the Emergency Recovery Disk (ERD) is used to recover from problems on systems that have already been installed.

For more information on this topic, see *A+ Exam Cram, 2nd Edition*, Chapter 13, the section "Active Directory".

What's on the CD-ROM

The A+ Practice Tests Exam Cram's companion CD-ROM contains the two Core Hardware and the two OS Technologies practice tests and answers from the book, plus a bonus Core Hardware and a bonus OS Technologies practice exam—all on our custom testing software.

When you combine the 280 questions from the book and the 140 bonus questions from the CD-ROM, you have 420 realistic practice questions in an interactive testing environment to help you prepare for the exam.

System Requirements

Software

➤ Your operating system must be Windows 98, 2000 or NT 4.

➤ Internet Explorer 5.x or above.

Hardware

➤ Minimum of a 486/66 MHz processor is recommended.

➤ 32MB RAM (64MB RAM recommended) is the minimum requirement.